Healthy cooking for children

52 brilliant ideas to dump the junk

Mandy Francis

brilliantideas

The right of Mandy Francis to be identified as the author of this book has been asserted in accordance with the Copyright, Designs and Patents Act 1988

First published in 2006 by
The Infinite Ideas Company Limited
36 St Giles
Oxford, OX1 3LD
United Kingdom
www.infideas.com

A CIP catalogue record for this book is available from the British Library

ISBN 1-904902-61-8

Brand and product names are trademarks or registered trademarks of their respective owners.

Designed by Baseline Arts Ltd, Oxford
Typeset by Sparks, Oxford
Printed in Italy

Brilliant ideas

Brilliant features

Each chapter of this book is designed to provide you with an inspirational idea that you can read quickly and put into practice straight away.

Throughout you'll find four features that will help you get right to the heart of the idea:

- *Here's an idea for you …* Take it on board and give it a go – right here, right now. Get an idea of how well you're doing so far.

- *Try another idea …* If this idea looks like a life-changer then there's no time to lose. *Try another idea …* will point you straight to a related tip to enhance and expand on the first.

- *Defining idea …* Words of wisdom from masters and mistresses of the art, plus some interesting hangers-on.

- *How did it go?* If at first you do succeed, try to hide your amazement. If, on the other hand, you don't, then this is where you'll find a Q and A that highlights common problems and how to get over them.

Introduction

Hands up! Who was sure, before their child was born, that they would provide him or her with the healthiest diet ever? And hands up – who is finding it a great deal more challenging than they ever imagined? Me too.

Without doubt, there is nothing better for your child than freshly prepared, home-cooked food. A balanced diet using lots of fresh ingredients will not only help your child to keep healthy now – but will also set him or her up to eat well for the rest of their lives. But finding the time, knowledge and confidence to do it can be daunting, I know.

Before I had my son Stanley – now almost four years old – and met my teenage step children, Christopher and Stephanie, I thought feeding children a healthy diet would be a pretty straightforward affair. But of course, it hasn't been. There's been weaning to cope with, fussy eating to deal with and my concerns about additives, salt and sugar. Then there are the times when I've just been too dog-tired to cook something healthy and the frustrations of waiting to see if yet another lovingly home-prepared meal will end up inside my child or scraped into the bin …

Through trial, error, research and dogged determination, however, I believe I've cracked it.

There are two main ideas behind this book, which I hope will provide you too with the knowledge and skills you need to feed your child well. The first is to offer simple answers to just about every nutritional dilemma and question you can think of.

The book is divided up into 52 simple, clear and concise chapters – so you can dip into it as and when you need, and hopefully find exactly what you're looking for immediately. If you're wondering what the best first foods to give your baby are, for example, or what your toddler should ideally be eating – the answers are here. If you'd like to find out how much salt he or she can have or you need ideas for nutritious packed lunches, this book is also the place to go.

If you're facing difficult times – your child wants to survive on smoky bacon crisps perhaps, or your teenager has suddenly decided to turn veggie – there are ideas to help you through and give you some inspiration too.

Much of the information in this book is based on the latest research findings from some of the top nutrition experts in the world as well as personal experience and the tried and tested advice of other parents and grandparents. I'm sure you'll turn to this book time and again for answers.

The other idea behind *Healthy Cooking for Children* is to offer lots of delicious, healthy recipes and meal suggestions – from nutritious baby purées to snacks and meals that will appeal to the whole family.

Busy parents need home cooking to be fast and easy, I know – I'm a working mum too – so many of the recipes in this book are deliberately simple and take about the same time as a microwave meal to prepare. Most are ideal for encouraging little helpers to get involved with cooking also. I hope that if you're stuck for ideas, a quick flick through the book will encourage you to try something new or remind you of a basic, well-loved family favourite you'd forgotten about. And if your child is addicted to chicken nuggets or burgers? Well, there are recipes for healthy, home-cooked versions of those too.

I've also included plenty of time and money-saving tricks in the book as well as practical advice on things like food storage and must-have kitchen gadgets. There's advice on shopping wisely and the basic ingredients no cook should be without. Then there's the fun stuff – ideas for catering for children's parties, picnics, cakes to bake, food your child can grow in a garden or window box and some unusual ways with their favourite naughty-but-nice food – chocolate.

When it comes to recipes, please note that all measurements are approximate conversions. For best results always follow just the metric or just the imperial measurements throughout the recipe – do not chop and change.

Finally, there are some people I need to thank and without whom this book could not have been written. Firstly, nutrition scientist Dr Hannah Theobald, who generously advised on the more technical chapters in the book. Secondly, the band of childminders who freely gave me the time, space and encouragement to write, including my partner Paul, my mother Jill, Alison, Theresa and Sharon. A big thank you is also due to my friend Linda, who suggested I write this book in the first place.

I really hope you enjoy reading and using this book as much as I did writing it. Feeding children a healthy diet can be easy if you stick to your guns and don't buy or offer them the stuff you'd rather they didn't eat. You'll need to be patient – but I promise you, with the confidence and know-how this book can give you, it is possible. You will see your son and daughter eat their greens.

Enjoy!

Mandy Francis

1
First foods

Think it might be time to start your child on solids? Wondering whether you should try baby rice or banana first?

Don't get stressed. This chapter will give you the confidence to make weaning easy — and fun.

When your baby stops getting all his nutrition from milk and starts eating some solid foods, he is considered to be weaned

It is currently recommended that you do not try to wean your baby until he is around six months (twenty-six weeks) old. At six months your baby should be able to sit up by himself, will have the tongue and mouth co-ordination needed to deal with food, and his digestion should be mature enough to cope with solids. If your baby was born prematurely, you should calculate six months from your baby's original due date, rather than the date on which he was born.

Of course, all babies are different, and some may be ready to start eating a more mixed diet much later or even slightly earlier than this.

It's important to note, however, that solid foods should never be introduced before four months. Feeding a baby solids too early can potentially damage his immature digestive system and may possibly contribute to a higher risk of developing allergic conditions such as eczema and asthma.

If you feel your baby is ready to eat before six months, talk to your health visitor, as there are some foods that are best avoided at this early stage – such as wheat, eggs, fish, shellfish, nuts, seeds and citrus fruit.

You can tell your baby is ready to try solid food when he:

- is able to sit up well in a high chair;
- shows an interest in your food;
- has started to hold objects and put them in his mouth;
- has gained a healthy weight (most babies are ready to eat solids when they've doubled their birth weight – around six months of age); and
- appears to be hungry – even though you have increased his milk feeds for a few days.

So what can you start with? Most parents start with a little baby rice, which is easily digested and one of the foods least likely to trigger an allergic reaction.

Defining idea...

'*Before I got married, I had six theories about bringing up children. Now I have six children and no theories.*'
JOHN WILMOT, 2nd Earl of Rochester (1647–1680)

Other foods you can try at six months include fruits, such as puréed banana, stewed and puréed pear or apple, and vegetables, such as cooked and puréed carrots, squash, broccoli, parsnips and cauliflower. You might also like to try starchy vegetables, such as potatoes, yam and sweet potato.

Peel all fruit and veg, remove any seeds, pips or core and steam or poach in unsalted water until soft. Salt and sugar should never be added to baby food. Once cooked, mash to a smooth pulp with a fork, use a mouli (a hand-held food mill), press through a sieve or blitz in a mini chopper for a really fine texture. You can use a little breast milk, formula or cooking water to loosen the purée.

You can start feeding your baby with a rubber-tipped baby spoon – but some experts recommend a clean finger. Simply dip your fingertip into the purée or cereal mixture and offer it to your baby. Don't expect him to eat very much – tiny tummies need really tiny portions, and most of his nutrition will continue to come from breast milk or formula for months to come. Do not add rice, cereals or any other foods to your baby's bottle or leave him alone with food – he could choke.

Jars of baby food are handy for travelling and emergencies, but making your own fruit and vegetable purées is much cheaper, less wasteful – and you'll know exactly what's in them. Most fresh fruit and vegetable purées will keep for a day in the fridge and, with the exception of banana, avocado, aubergine and melon, will freeze well in small pots or ice cube trays. Just heat through really thoroughly and allow to cool before serving.

Here's an idea for you…

It's a good idea to offer just one food at a time so that you can check for any adverse reaction. It's also important you offer your baby savoury foods as well as sweet at this stage, to stop him developing a sweet tooth.

Your child will be learning about tastes and textures as he goes – so let him explore and 'feed' himself with his fingers and the spoon if

Adding meat, fish or vegetarian protein to your baby's diet is the next stage – turn to IDEA 3, *Ankle biters*, to find out how.

Try another idea…

3

he wants. Don't try and force your baby to eat if he's not interested – let him move at his own pace. And don't worry if he's a slow starter, he'll still be getting plenty of nutrients from his breast milk or formula feeds.

As your baby starts to eat more solid foods, he will take less milk. Milk is still an important part of your baby's diet, however. Carry on breastfeeding or giving infant formula every day until he is at least twelve months old. Cows' milk is not suitable as a drink until after twelve months, but you can use it in cooking or offer foods like yogurt, fromage frais, cheese and custard from six months onwards.

How did it go?

Q My baby is happy to eat fruit purées, but I'm having real trouble interesting her in savoury foods. Any tips?

A *Babies naturally prefer sweet tastes, as breast milk and formula contain milk sugars. You should persist with savoury foods, however, but never force your baby to eat anything. Try purées of naturally sweet vegetables like carrot, swede, sweet potato and parsnip. Alternatively, try mixing savoury with sweet – carrot and apple, for example, or mashed banana and avocado.*

Q Can I add a touch of honey or sugar to savoury dishes, just to make them more palatable?

A *Honey should not be given to children under twelve months at all, as it can sometimes contain a bacterial spore that can cause a rare and serious form of food poisoning (botulism) in babies. Wait until your child is at least one year old before giving him honey. You should not add sugar to babies' food either as it can damage teeth and encourage a sweet tooth.*

2

Keep it clean

Babies are especially vulnerable to the bacteria that can cause food poisoning , so here are some top tips for keeping tummy upsets at bay.

It's vital to store, prepare and cook food correctly if you want to keep your child healthy.

The following advice might seem a bit scary and serious – but it really is important to adopt good food hygiene habits when there's a baby in the house. The following tips will help to keep your family and you happy and healthy for years to come.

KITCHEN CLEANLINESS

- Keeping bacteria at bay means wiping all the places your baby eats or plays as clean as possible. Wipe over her high chair with an appropriate disinfectant/ antibacterial cleanser before she eats – and try and keep floors clean too.
- Washing your hands before and during food preparation is one of the best ways to prevent the spread of bacteria that cause food poisoning. Make sure you wash hands thoroughly with soap and warm water (water alone is not enough) and dry them carefully, because bacteria spread more easily when hands are damp. Use disposable kitchen towels or a clean hand towel to dry them, not a tea towel.
- The most hygienic way to wash up is in the dishwasher, as the high temperatures will kill bacteria. Otherwise, wash utensils, crockery and so on under

a running hot tap, using antibacterial washing-up liquid. Damp and reused kitchen cloths can harbour and spread all kinds of nasties so, again, use kitchen paper or a clean dry cloth.

■ Milk residue in bottles, teats or beakers is a breeding ground for bacteria. Baby bottles and feeding equipment should be thoroughly sterilised until your child is at least six months old.

■ Keep nappies away from food preparation and serving areas and always wash your hands after handling them.

Beware of cross-contamination

Another major cause of food poisoning is cross-contamination – the transfer of germs from one food (usually raw) to another. The germs can be transferred directly, when one food touches or drips onto another, or indirectly from hands, kitchen equipment, work surfaces, knives and other utensils.

To prevent cross-contamination:

■ Wash your hands thoroughly immediately after touching raw food.

■ Always keep raw and ready-to-eat foods separate. Use different chopping boards or work surfaces for raw food and ready-to-eat food. Never cut bread, vegetables, fruit or any other foods on a board or use a knife that has had raw meat on it previously.

■ Wash knives and other utensils thoroughly after using with raw food.

■ Use rigid plastic chopping boards rather than wood – they're easier to clean and more hygienic.

Here's an idea for you... **To store food safely, your fridge temperature should be below 5°C. Freezers should be below -18°C. You can buy fridge and freezer thermometers quite cheaply to monitor the temperature.**

■ Store food safely. Cover foods in the fridge. Store raw and cooked foods separately: raw foods in the bottom of the fridge and cooked foods at the top.

Food preparation

■ Frozen food should be properly thawed before you cook them thoroughly. Defrost foods in a cool place, preferably in the fridge. Do not thaw them in a warm room.

To find out more about the best way to store foods long term, turn to IDEA 51 The Big Freeze

Try another idea…

■ Always make sure that food, particularly meat and poultry, is kept cold in the fridge – or heated thoroughly to piping hot before cooling to serving temperature. Don't assume that the instructions on the packaging will be sufficient, because ovens vary. If meat is properly cooked, the centre shouldn't be pink and the juices should run clear when the meat is pierced at the centre of its thickest part with a skewer (make sure the skewer is clean each time you use it).

■ Small children are particularly vulnerable to salmonella poisoning, so always cook eggs until they are hard all the way through. Scrambled egg should contain no liquid.

■ Always stir microwaved food to check that it is piping hot in the middle.

Food storage

■ Don't store food in opened cans – always decant it into a sealable container and put it in the fridge.

■ Bacteria like it warm, so take chilled and frozen foods home as quickly as possible from the supermarket and put them back into a fridge or freezer immediately. Keep-

'Cleanliness and order are not matters of instinct; they are matters of education, and like most great things, you must cultivate a taste for them.'
BENJAMIN DISRAELI, British prime minister and novelist (1804–1881)

Defining idea…

ing an insulated freezer bag in your car to ferry cold foods between shop and home is a good idea, particularly in warm weather.

■ Always check the dates on food and use within the recommended period.
■ Do not leave leftovers at room temperature – allow to cool, then cover and place in the fridge and use within 24 hours (see How Did It Go? for further, vital advice on leftovers).

And finally, the golden rule – if you are even the tiniest bit uncertain about serving something to your baby – don't.

How did it go?

Q   My baby eats so little at the moment, I always end up with a sub-stantial amount of leftover food in her bowl. Is it OK to cover it with cling film and keep it in the fridge until the next meal?

A   *Definitely not. Traces of saliva will contaminate the food. I suggest you just heat up much smaller portions each time instead. It's also a very bad idea to reheat food more than once.*

Q   What about jars of baby food then – does that mean I have to discard the whole jar if I just use a little of it?

A   *No, not unless you've warmed up the entire jar or have been feeding your child directly from it – in which case, I'm afraid it does have to go in the bin. If you just take the amount that you need from the jar with a clean spoon and heat it up separately, however, you can decant the rest into a clean, covered bowl and store it in the fridge for 24 hours.*

3

Ankle biters

If your baby appears to be actively enjoying solids it's time to introduce more variety and, ultimately, more texture to his diet.

Your baby is over six months, you've started him on solids and he seems to be relishing his tiny portions of mashed banana, carrot purée and baby rice. Here's what you can try next.

Feeds will still be mainly breast or formula milk, but when you're both ready, you can start to gradually increase the variety and amount of solid food you give, either before, during, or after his milk feed.

You will need to be really, really patient, however, and go at your baby's pace. Never rush or force feed him. Instead, respond to his appetite, giving a little more food as and when he wants it. At the same time, you can start to move from offering solids during or after just one milk feed in the day to solid food with two, and then three feeds.

WHAT SHOULD HE BE EATING NOW?

Once he's truly got the hang of solids, you can also start adding other foods to the vegetable, fruit and cereal purées that you are already giving, such as:

- Puréed meat and poultry.
- Puréed lentils.
- Full-fat milk products such as yoghurt, fromage frais.
- Full-fat cows' milk can also be used for cooking, for example in cheese sauce and custard, but avoid giving cows' milk to your baby as a drink until after he is a year old.

Try to give cereals such as baby rice to your child just once a day, then use mashed-up, sieved or puréed family food when you can. Offer a wide variety of different foods, as this might help to avoid picky eating later on. Your baby should still be having at least 600ml/1 pint breast milk or formula a day.

Foods to avoid:

Here's an idea for you...

It's quite common for babies to throw food and upturn bowls – so keep your nerve if this starts to happen. Most children do it because they know it will get them your full attention. The best tack is to take a deep breath, try not to react, and calmly clear up and start again if necessary. Buy bowls with suction cups on the bottom and cover the floor with a splash mat or newspaper for some damage limitation.

- Eggs.
- Anything that salt has been added to. (Remember to keep an eye on the number of high salt foods in your baby's diet such as cheese, bacon and sausages too.)
- Sugary foods and anything containing honey.
- Processed foods that have not been specifically designed for babies. Always read ingredients lists carefully and, if you're in doubt, avoid the product.

Only warm up really small portions of food at a time – you can always go for seconds if your baby seems hungry for more. Never put half-eaten leftovers back in the fridge or refreeze as they will have been contaminated with saliva.

For advice on making purées and freezing them in small quantities turn to IDEA 51, The big freeze.

Try another idea...

ONE LUMP OR TWO?

As your baby's appetite continues to develop, adjust the texture of foods to a slightly thicker consistency to encourage him to learn to chew and manage small pieces of food – even if he hasn't developed teeth yet. Try finger foods too, such as toast, breadsticks, pitta bread, banana, cooked carrot sticks and green beans, or tiny cubes of cheese. Ideally your baby should have one serving of protein, such as soft, cooked meat, fish, well-cooked egg, tofu or pulses – no matter how small that portion is – every day.

Always stay near your baby during feeding to give encouragement and to make sure that he doesn't choke.

As your baby becomes increasingly used to eating solid foods, he should be learning to fit in with the family by eating three minced or chopped meals, plus a minimum of 600ml/1 pint breast or formula milk throughout the day as the main drink. Give him fruit or other healthy snacks between meals.

If your baby is on the move (he may have started crawling), you may find you need to increase the amount of food you give. Babies have small stomachs and they need lots of energy to grow, so make sure any dairy products you give are full-fat.

'You can learn many things from children. How much patience you have, for instance.'

FRANKLIN P. JONES

Defining idea...

11

Encourage your baby to learn to feed himself too. If he shows an interest, give him a spoon to experiment with whilst you feed him. Just be prepared for some mess!

How did it go?

Q   There seem to be lots of sweet biscuits and rusks around that are specially designed for babies – you don't mention them. Why?

A   *It's best to avoid giving your child sweet biscuits and rusks, so that she doesn't get into the habit of expecting sweet snacks all the time.*

Q   My baby has only got a couple of teeth. Should I start cleaning them now that she's on solids?

A   *Babies' teeth should be cleaned at least once a day as soon as there is sufficient tooth surface showing – and whether she's on solids or not. At first you may find it easier to use a piece of clean gauze wrapped around your forefinger to do this. Later use a small, soft baby toothbrush with a tiny amount of baby toothpaste and massage it around baby's gums and teeth. Once your toddler shows an interest in trying to clean her own teeth let her have a go, showing her how to brush up and down, rather than from side to side. However, remember that you will need to continue finishing off the brushing process for some years to come, as a child does not have the manual dexterity to clean teeth thoroughly until she's about seven years old.*

4
Veggie mites

Raising a vegetarian baby requires careful planning to ensure that all nutritional needs are met during this time of rapid growth and development.

Because we all want the best for our children, it's vital to know that whilst a vegetarian diet can be a healthy option for a small baby, there are special considerations to bear in mind.

Firstly you will need to ensure that once she gets to grips with solids and can manage a more varied diet she must eat foods from the following food groups every day:

- Cereals.
- Milk and dairy products.
- Nuts and seeds (foods containing nuts should not be given before six months, whole nuts should not be given before five years of age).
- Pulses, beans and soya products.

Here's an idea for you...

From six months the iron stores your baby was born with will be starting to run out. So, you need to start offering him extra iron-rich foods. Iron can be more difficult to obtain from a vegetarian diet as haem iron (which is the type of iron that is best absorbed) is found only in red meat. Ensure vegetarian sources of iron such as pulses and dark green vegetables are given every day along with foods or drinks containing vitamin C to help your baby absorb the iron from them.

If your baby is a fussy eater, dislikes the texture or taste of some of the recommended food groups or has a food allergy, then you should seek advice from a registered dietician. Your GP should be able to refer you to one.

The nutrients that are particularly important to include in your baby's vegetarian diet include iron, vitamin B12 and protein.

Iron can be found in fortified breakfast cereals, dark green vegetables, green beans and peas, dried fruit, nuts, eggs, and pulses, including baked beans and soya products.

Vitamin B12 sources include fortified breakfast cereals, low-salt yeast extract, eggs, milk and dairy products.

Breast milk and formula are also good sources of vitamin B12 and your baby should continue to have at least 600ml/1 pint breast milk or formula (or both) until at least her first birthday.

Rich sources of protein include eggs, milk and dairy products, nuts and pulses (including baked beans), soya and soya products. Bread, cereals, rice and pasta can also contain useful amounts of protein.

So which foods should you offer and when?

It is now recommended that you aim to feed your baby on breast milk or infant formula until she is six months old, then gradually introduce solids whilst continuing with breast or formula milk as her main drink.

For advice on weaning see IDEA 1, *First foods*; and to find out more about feeding older vegetarian children read IDEA 33, *Vegging out*.

Try another idea…

Do not start solids before four months as your baby's digestive system is not yet mature enough to cope with solid food and do not give wheat, oats, milk, nuts, eggs or citrus fruit before the age of six months.

Assuming you start your baby on solids at six months, below is a rough guide to the types of food you should offer – and when.

- 6–7 months. Start with 1 teaspoon of food once a day just before or during a milk feed. Suitable foods include baby rice mixed with expressed breast milk or formula milk. Puréed fruit – apple, pear, banana, peach. Puréed vegetables – potato, sweet potato, carrot, spinach, broccoli.
- 7–8 months. Start to gradually increase the amount of solids given to two then three times per day. Continue with the foods already offered and add iron-rich foods such as puréed lentils and dark green vegetables.
- 8–10 months. You can now start to give her wheat, oats, tofu, smooth nut butters, mashed beans and pulses, well-cooked eggs and dairy products, such as cheese, custard, yogurt and fromage frais, (cows' milk should not be introduced as a main drink until she is 12 months old). Nutrient-rich foods like milk, cheese and eggs will help ensure the diet isn't too bulky but that your baby still gets plenty of calcium, zinc and vitamin A.

'I've been a vegetarian for years and years. I'm not judgemental about others who aren't, I just feel I cannot eat or wear living creatures.'
DREW BARRYMORE,
American actress

Defining idea…

15

■ 10–14 months. Start offering baby finger foods, such as cooked carrots and green beans, breadsticks and slivers of cheese squares. Mashed up family food can also be given, so long as it does not contain added salt.

How did it go?

Q   Can I give my baby Quorn and textured vegetable protein (TVP)?

A   *Quorn and TVP are best introduced once your child is at least two years old. This is because they are both relatively low in calories and high in fibre, so may satisfy your baby's appetite before enough energy has been taken in. If you want to give Quorn or TVP occasionally which, of course, won't do any harm – always check the sodium content first, as some products may contain salt.*

Q   Can I wean my baby on a vegan diet?

A   *A vegan diet is much more restricted than a vegetarian diet as it also excludes milk, dairy products and eggs. Some vegans will not eat anything of animal origin at all, including honey, and many other animal derivatives. It may be possible to wean your baby as a vegan, as long as you make absolutely sure that a broad variety of nutrient-rich foods are included. Vegan babies need good sources of calcium, vitamin B12, vitamin D and protein. Ask your GP, health visitor or a registered dietician for advice.*

5
I think I'm going to be sick!

Don't panic about food allergies and intolerances – there are simple ways to minimise the risks and reactions.

Whether it's nut allergies or dairy and gluten sensitivities — sometimes feeding children can feel as if you're negotiating a minefield of potential food nightmares. This simple guide explains the basics.

It's a fact of life that food intolerances and allergies are much more common in babies and children up to the age of five than in any other age group. Official estimates suggest up to 7% of children under the age of five may be affected by a food intolerance at some time and 1–2% by a true allergy.

The most common food allergies and intolerances are:

- cows' milk,
- egg,
- nuts,

- wheat,
- gluten (a protein found in wheat, rye, barley and possibly oats),
- fish,
- shellfish,
- citrus fruits,
- tomatoes,
- sesame seeds, and
- soya.

So what is the difference between a food allergy and a food intolerance?

A true food allergy will usually cause an immediate reaction after eating a particular food. Symptoms can occur a few seconds or minutes after eating. The most common symptoms are itchy skin, itchy or swelling tongue and lips, sneezing, blocked or runny nose, shortness of breath and coughing.

The most severe form of allergy is called anaphylaxis. This is a potentially life-threatening allergic reaction that requires emergency medical treatment. Symptoms may include an itchy skin rash (hives), swelling of the lips and tongue, tightening of the throat, difficulty breathing and feeling faint. Your child may look pale and clammy. Left untreated, an anaphylactic reaction may cause loss of consciousness and, in rare circumstances, may be fatal. If you suspect your child may be having an anaphylactic attack, phone 999 or go straight to casualty.

Here's an idea for you... **When weaning your child it's always a good idea to offer just one new food at a time so that you can check for any adverse reactions.**

For further information visit the anaphylaxis campaign website www.anaphylaxis.org.uk. The telephone helpline is 01252 542029

For more detailed advice on weaning go to IDEA 1, *First foods.*

Try another idea...

A food intolerance gives a much more delayed reaction, often occurring hours or even days after eating certain foods. It will often involve digestive problems of some kind. Symptoms may include tummy pain or colic, bloating, wind, diarrhoea, and sometimes vomiting. A food intolerance can cause a lot of discomfort and over time, malnutrition, but it is not life-threatening.

It's important to note, however, that there are quite a few other conditions that have similar symptoms to food intolerance – so never just assume your child has a food intolerance and try to deal with it yourself. If you think there's a problem, always pay a visit to your GP for a proper diagnosis.

Children with a family history of allergy are most susceptible to an allergic reaction or intolerance, but because not every child who experiences an intolerance or allergy has a family history of allergy, all parents are advised to avoid giving foods that commonly cause reactions until specific age milestones.

None of the foods mentioned in the list here, for example, should be given before six months – and children should never be weaned onto solids before four months. In fact current recommendations suggest chil-

'Variety's the very spice of life, that gives it all its flavour.'
WILLIAM COWPER, British writer and poet (1731–1800)

Defining idea...

dren should ideally not start on solids at all until they are around six months old. If you feel your baby is ready for solids earlier, ask your health visitor for advice, just to be on the safe side.

Cows' milk should not be given as a drink until after twelve months – but you can, providing your child shows no reaction to it, use it in cooking or offer foods like yogurt, fromage frais, cheese and custard from six months onwards. Nuts, in the form of nut butters, soft and blue cheeses, shellfish, raw or lightly cooked eggs are also all best left out of your child's diet until he's at least a year old. (NB It is recommended that you wait until your child is five years old before giving nuts as they are very easy to choke on.)

The good news is, many children do eventually go on to outgrow their food allergies and intolerances. Up to 90% of children will outgrow cows' milk and egg allergies, and cows' milk protein intolerance, for example, while 10–20% may outgrow nut allergies.

In the meantime, if an allergy or intolerance is diagnosed, you will probably have to become an expert at reading food labels. Meals, parties and snacks will take a bit more planning and organisation, but with the wide choice of specialist foods available these days, and a greater public awareness of allergy and intolerance it doesn't have to be a nightmare. You will soon get used to providing suitable food and drinks for your child or advising others on how to do the same.

Q **This all sounds a bit scary! I'm worrying about offering my eight-month-old new foods now.**

How did it go?

A *Please don't panic – and don't start avoiding hundreds of foods because you're scared of an adverse reaction. If you follow the guidelines, your baby has a much higher chance of not developing an adverse reaction to any food at all. It's actually far more important to encourage your child to eat the widest possible range of foods for optimal nutrition and to avoid her becoming a fussy eater.*

Q **I noticed my local healthfood shop is offering allergy testing – is it worth me taking my daughter along to find out if she might be allergic to anything?**

A *No. The types of test offered in health food shops are not suitable. If you are worried that your daughter is allergic to something – or concerned about her diet – go and see your GP right away. Your GP will be able to advise you and, if necessary, may refer your daughter to a recognised dermatology or allergy clinic for a specialist skin prick test and/or a blood test.*

6

Choose your weapons

There are hundreds of gadgets and gimmicks designed to help with the weaning process – but which ones are really worth buying?

The following lists of essential feeding aids, handy cooking equipment and clever tips really will help to make feeding your baby much easier.

FEEDING ESSENTIALS

- *Suction bowl*. Forget matching cartoon crockery. Your best buy is a baby bowl with a suction cup underneath. It will stay put – an advantage that any mother who has cleared carrot purée from the recesses of a high chair, her lap and the kitchen floor will truly appreciate.
- *Shallow, rubber-tipped baby spoons*. Just the right size for a baby's small mouth and appetite – she can also wield one of these with abandon, without damaging her teeth and gums.
- *Drink beaker*. Although she may still be breastfeeding or taking her milk from a bottle your baby will be ready to try drinking from a beaker at mealtimes from around six months. Buy a spill-proof beaker with handles and a soft spout, and

put expressed milk, infant formula or boiled and cooled water in it. (Discard any leftover milk as soon as possible and sterilise as you would a baby bottle. Bacteria that stick to milk curds can be dangerous.) Even if she doesn't want to drink from it at first – you can present it at mealtimes so she can start getting used to the idea.

■ *Bibs.* Bibs are a must at weaning time. Terry towelling bibs with velcro fastenings are best as they're easy to put on and take off and soft enough to use to wipe your child's face as she feeds. If you can find the long version that reaches right down to your baby's lap – even better. Tie bibs can be fiddly. Plastic bibs with a lip at the bottom tend to be hot, restrictive and uncomfortable – disposable paper bibs too lightweight and easy to screw up into a ball.

Here's an idea for you...

A highchair with a tray is the best place to start weaning and encouraging your child to feed himself. Most babies will be ready to sit in a highchair from around six months, but let your child guide you. Wait until he's sitting up well with a strong back and good head and neck control. Many highchairs come with a booster cushion to stop smaller children sliding about. Make sure you strap your child in properly – and never leave him unattended in the chair – particularly if he has food in front of him.

REALLY USEFUL COOKING EQUIPMENT

■ Mouli. If you want to cook from fresh on a regular basis, a mouli is a really handy and relatively inexpensive investment. Useful for puréeing small amounts of fruit and vegetables, this hand-operated food mill will get rid of seeds, fruit skins and so on – and produce a nice smooth texture. You can buy one from a cook shop, large department store or online.

■ Electric blender or food processor. A regular kitchen blender or food processor is essential if you plan to purée large quantities of food for freezing. If you don't already own a blender and are short on kitchen and cupboard space, then a compact hand-held stick blender with a tall plastic beaker is a good buy. If you're keen to cook on a daily basis however, some regular blenders have baby blender attachments that you can use to process smaller quantities of food. Alternatively, put a baby food blender on your present list – you can always use it for processing herbs, nuts and bread crumbs when baby outgrows it.

Scrupulous hygiene is essential at this age if tummy upsets are to be avoided. Read IDEA 2, *Keep it clean*, for the best advice.

Try another idea…

- Steamer. Steaming foods helps to preserve nutrients and taste, so it's a good idea to have one of these, particularly for cooking vegetables before puréeing. Unless you're sure you'll use it for family dishes too, a tiered electric steamer is unnecessary. A simple metal steamer that fits on or in a saucepan is much cheaper and will do the job just as well.
- Small, non-stick milk saucepan. Great for cooking small quantities of anything quickly.
- Fine sieve. By this, I mean the kind of metal or plastic sieve you would use to sieve flour through. Invaluable for straining tiny pieces of veg and pasta (they tend to fall through the holes on a conventional colander) – you can also push mashed fruit and veg through it with the back of a spoon to get a nice fine purée.
- Ice cube trays. Weaning can be a really wasteful business if you're not careful, as babies do eat very little to begin with. Cooking up a batch of food and freezing it in ice cube trays (once frozen, tip the food cubes into a sealed plastic bag and label with the name of the food and the date) is a great way to have small portions of home-cooked food to hand.

'Even when freshly washed and relieved of all obvious confections, children tend to be sticky.'
FRAN LEBOWITZ, American journalist

Defining idea…

Q **I've been sitting my seven-month-old son in a highchair and using a suction bowl and a bib as you suggest – but we still manage to get food absolutely everywhere. Any other suggestions to minimise the mess?**

       A *A wipe-clean, plastic splash mat that you stand the highchair on is a handy investment to protect your floor from splatters. Alternatively you could use sheets of newspaper. Kitchen roll and a pack of disposable floor wipes are also a good idea, as you can wipe up the goo in one go and chuck the whole lot away.*

       Q **But what about all those annoying bits of cereal, toast crumbs, raisins and so on? I'm fed up with getting the hoover out after every meal.**

       A *I found a small, hand-held vacuum cleaner an absolute godsend. But do buy the most powerful one you can afford, as the cheaper versions are often ineffective.*

7

The white stuff

Follow-on formula, cows' milk, semi-skimmed or full fat? How much milk and how often? You'll find the answers here.

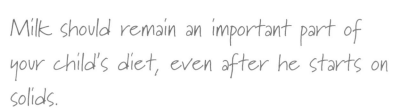

Milk should remain an important part of your child's diet, even after he starts on solids.

The Department of Health recommends breast milk or infant formula for babies up to the age of twelve months. After that time, full fat cows' milk may be given instead.

Cows' milk is not suitable for babies under six months old, because their immature digestive systems are unable to process the protein and salt that it contains. Cows' milk is not currently recommended for babies under the age of one year either, as it is low in iron and vitamin C – two nutrients essential to growing babies.

From twelve months onwards, however, milk should still play an important role in your baby's diet, as it provides essential calcium, protein, vitamins and minerals. Ideally, your toddler needs to have a minimum of 350ml (⅔ pint) of full fat cows' milk each day until he's two years old.

Here's an idea for you... **If your child goes off milk drinks before she reaches her second birthday – try offering two portions of calcium-rich foods a day to top up her diet. Yoghurt, cheese, tinned mashed sardines and fortified white bread all contain useful levels of calcium.**

Full fat cows' milk should be given to your baby until he is two years old in preference to skimmed or semi-skimmed, because your child still needs the energy that the fat in milk provides to grow. The fat in the milk also helps to carry essential vitamins A and D. After he reaches his second birthday you can swap down to semi-skimmed milk if you wish.

OTHER TYPES OF MILK – WHEN AND WHY?

- Follow-on milk is a formula milk with a higher protein and mineral content than regular infant formula. It is suitable for babies over six months old, and advertised as being more nutritious than cows' milk. It's not essential, however. Most experts recommend meeting your child's increasing nutritional needs as he grows with more of his standard formula, plus calcium and iron-rich foods. That said, the ready-made cartons of follow-on milk, which don't need refrigerating unless opened, can be handy for travelling and days out.
- Soya-based formula is made from soya beans, which are modified for use in formula with vitamins, minerals and nutrients. Babies should only be given soya-based formula on the advice of a health professional, such as a health visitor, GP or dietician.
- Goats' milk is not suitable for babies – and infant formulas and follow-on formulas based on goats' milk have not been approved for use in Europe. There is a belief that infant formula and follow-on formula based on goats' milk protein are suitable alternatives for babies who are intolerant or allergic to cows' milk formulas. However, some of the proteins in goats' milk are similar to those found in cows' milk and most babies that react to cows' milk protein are also likely to react to goats' milk protein. Since the levels of lactose are similar in

both milks, formulas derived from goats' milk are also unsuitable for babies that are lactose-intolerant.

What should your child be eating once she's weaned? Find out in IDEA 8, *Up and running.*

Try another idea…

COWS' MILK INTOLERANCE AND ALLERGY

Around 1–3% of all babies will develop a cows' milk intolerance or allergy. Symptoms include persistent crying, weight loss or no weight gain, reflux, vomiting, colic, burping, flatulence, diarrhoea, constipation, skin rashes and shortness of breath. If your child has any of these symptoms see your GP immediately for a diagnosis.

Cows' milk intolerance is an intolerance to either milk protein or lactose, a sugar found in cows' milk. Tests need to be done to establish whether the child has a milk protein or lactose intolerance. If your baby has an intolerance of cows' milk protein he may still be able to have some cows' milk and cows' milk products.

Lactose intolerance is caused by lactase deficiency, the enzyme in the body that digests milk. If lactase deficiency is diagnosed, your baby might be put on a low lactose diet which may allow low lactose milk and milk products.

If your baby is found to have a cows' milk protein allergy, rather than a simple intolerance, cows' milk and associated products will have to be excluded from his diet completely.

The good news is, up to 90% of children will eventually outgrow their cows' milk allergies, and cows' milk protein intolerance.

'There are three reasons for breast-feeding: the milk is always at the right temperature; it comes in attractive containers; and the cat can't get it.'
IRENA CHALMERS, American cookery writer and publisher

Defining idea…

29

How did it go?

Q   My baby's seven months old now and I want to give up breast-feeding. I know cows' milk is unsuitable until she is one – so should I give her formula in a bottle?

A   *If you wean your baby from the breast when she is six months or more, you may be able to bypass bottles completely. The sucking action required for breast or bottle feeding is not as necessary to your baby now as it was when she was younger. She should be able to take most of her drinks from a feeder cup, or beaker. She may, however, still prefer to have a bottle – or breastfeed last thing at night for comfort.*

Q   What sort of beaker are we talking about?

A   *It's best to start with a spill-proof beaker with a soft spout. You'll find plenty of different styles in your local pharmacy or supermarket. You could use expressed milk in it at first to get her used to it before you swap to formula.*

Q   Why is a beaker preferable to a bottle and teat?

A   *Experts recommend transferring to a cup because using a bottle, especially as a comforter, can damage teeth, as drinks are swilled around the mouth for long periods of time.*

8

Up and running

The pre-school years are when the foundations for balanced eating and future good health are laid.

Now weaning is over you've reached a crucial time in your child's dietary development.

A child's diet needs careful handling now. She needs lots of nutrients and energy, but her appetite is likely to be small, and she may be a bit fussy about her food. Small, frequent and nutrient-dense meals are the order of the day.

The best foods for your pre-school child are divided into four main groups and a fifth or 'occasional' group. If you base your child's diet on these groups you can be certain that she'll be getting all the important nutrients she needs at this age.

GROUP 1: STARCHY CARBOHYDRATES

Some bread, rice, pasta, cereals and potatoes should be served with all meals. An average portion of starchy carbohydrates for a pre-school child might be one slice of bread or two tablespoons of cereal, pasta or rice or a small baked potato.

- Vary the way you serve potatoes and the types of bread you offer – think granary, rolls, pittas, chapattis, bagels and breadsticks.
- Buy interesting pasta shapes to encourage your child to eat well.

■ Serve fortified breakfast cereals (those that have added vitamins and minerals) or porridge first thing.

GROUP 2: FRUIT AND VEGETABLES

These should also be eaten often. Aim for five portions a day. A portion of fruit for a child of this age would be a small whole fruit or half a large fruit (e.g. half a large apple, orange or pear), two tablespoons of berries or eight grapes. A portion of vegetables would be one to two heaped tablespoons of cooked veg or two broccoli florets or a small sliced carrot.

■ Fruit makes a great dessert or snack – ring the changes often.
■ Don't forget to offer vegetable crudités for snacks.
■ Frozen and tinned fruit and vegetables can be just as nutritious as fresh varieties. Look for fruit tinned in juice and 'reduced sugar and salt' tinned vegetables.
■ If vegetables aren't popular, try hiding them by blending them into soups, sauces, casseroles and pizzas.

Here's an idea for you... **One UK study showed that you may have to offer a new food eight to ten times before your pre-school child will accept it. Present it in tiny amounts – and don't give up!**

GROUP 3: MILK AND DAIRY PRODUCTS

An important source of calcium and energy. Aim for at least three portions of dairy products a day. A portion of dairy products would be 200ml milk, 30g hard or soft cheese or a small pot of yogurt or fromage frais.

■ Use full fat milk and dairy products. Semi-skimmed milk can be given from the age of two if the overall diet contains enough energy.
■ Milk shakes and yogurt smoothies made with real fruit make a healthy snack or small meal.

- Cheese can be quite high in salt, so a little can be made to go a long way. Use it grated over baked potatoes, in sandwiches, on toast and over spaghetti and omelettes
- Flavoured yogurts can be high in added sugar and additives, so try natural yogurt and add fruit purée to sweeten.

Many pre-school children go through phases of refusing to eat certain foods or refusing to eat anything at all. Read IDEA 11, *Fussy eaters*, for advice.

Try another idea…

GROUP 4: MEAT, FISH AND VEGETARIAN PROTEIN ALTERNATIVES

These should be eaten twice a day. A portion would be 40–50g cooked meat, fish, poultry or pulses or one whole egg.

- Large pieces of meat can be off-putting for children, so keep portions small. Minced beef, turkey, chicken, pork, shepherd's pie, meatballs and spaghetti Bolognese are all ideal – use lean cuts and mince.
- Mashed sardines, salmon, tuna, cold meat slices and patés are great sandwich fillers.
- Make your own chicken nuggets, fish cakes and fish fingers.
- Eggs should be thoroughly cooked – either boiled, in sandwiches, as omelettes, poached or scrambled.
- Try different beans and pulses, such as lentils, baked beans, peas and chickpeas. Mash them in a dip or use them in casseroles, soups and bean burgers.

GROUP 5: FATTY AND SUGARY FOODS

This includes spreading fats, cooking oils, sugar, biscuits, cakes, crisps, sweets, chocolate, cream, ice cream and sugary drinks. These

'Experiencing food problems is a normal and common stage of development in pre-school children. One third of under-5s practise food refusal or selective eating.'
The Royal College of Psychiatrists

Defining idea…

33

shouldn't be given too often and when they are, only in small amounts. Too many servings from this group can affect your child's intake of more nutritious foods.

How did it go?

Q My son refuses to eat red meat. Can he get iron from elsewhere?

A   *Iron-deficiency is common in this age group as iron requirements are high but dietary intake is often low, especially if little or no meat is eaten. Meat contains haem iron that is easily absorbed by the body.*

Other reasonable sources of dietary iron such as chick peas, baked beans (choose the reduced sugar and salt variety), dried apricots, spinach, wholegrain cereals and bread – and to a lesser extent, eggs – contain what is known as non-haem iron. Non-haem iron foods need to be eaten with a vitamin C-rich food to maximise iron absorption, so give your son diluted orange juice or fruit for dessert with meals containing these foods.

Q My three-year-old refuses to eat very much at all at meal times. What can I do to encourage him?

A   *Young children have small appetites – so it's important to keep meals small and energy dense. A mountain of food can be off-putting. Don't give too many hefty snacks in between meals, either – try and stick to fruit and vegetable batons, milk, water and diluted fruit juice. Making his meal as attractive and 'fun' as possible might help too. Buy bright plates, bowls, forks and spoons and use interesting pasta shapes, draw faces in the food, give the meal a funny name. Don't worry – his appetite for more sizeable meals will increase with age.*

9
Let them eat greens

If you're struggling to get your child to eat one portion of veg a day – let alone the recommended three – don't despair, there are some relatively simple ways to get him to eat more of the good stuff.

So just what is it about vegetables that makes so many children refuse to eat them?

There are many reasons why your child may be making such a fuss over his greens. But the good news is, there are also lots of ways you can encourage him to change his habits.

A BID FOR INDEPENDENCE

Refusing to eat certain foods, especially those the parent wants him to eat, makes a small child feel independent and grown up. This is very common behaviour between the ages of five and six, but can also be true of older children.

If this sounds like your child, try not to make a big deal of his refusal to eat veg and, instead, look for other ways for him to exercise control in his life. Small children could start choosing what to wear every day; older children could be allowed to decide their bedtime on a weekend night, for example.

EXPRESSING ANGER

By rejecting food a parent has worked hard to prepare, a small child could be expressing anger or resentment that he cannot put into words.

Perhaps he hasn't had enough attention lately? Maybe you have chastised or punished him for something he feels is just not fair? This type of food rejection is likely to be accompanied by tears and tantrums.

If this sounds like the stand-off in your home, think about what might be the cause of the underlying emotional distress and try to address it.

Here's an idea for you... **Use root vegetables such as sweet potato, parsnips, uncooked beetroot and swede to make unusual (and slightly sweet) vegetable crisps. Slice the vegetables thinly, toss in a little oil, and lay out – without overlapping – on a baking tray. Bake in a pre-heated oven at 190C/375F/Gas 5 for 20 minutes, then flip your crisps over and bake for a further 10–15 minutes until cooked.**

PLAYING COPYCAT

Younger siblings will often copy their older brothers and sisters. So if your older children are being awkward about eating their veggies – the younger one might start too. Stay relaxed and neutral. Continue to serve vegetables at every meal and ignore any rejection. The fad will quickly pass if it doesn't get a reaction.

To ensure that your child really does end up eating his greens – try the following tips too:

- Don't make compromises. Only buy and serve the foods that you want your child to eat.
- Eat vegetables yourself to set the right example.
- Many children may not like eating cooked vegetables – but will eat them raw. Try carrot batons, baby sweetcorn, fresh peas in pods, celery and sweet red pepper strips.
- Remember veggies don't have to be green. Offer brightly coloured alternatives such as sweetcorn, peppers, sweet potatoes and swede. You can use them to garnish a dish and make it look more exciting.
- Let your child help to plan menus, shop for, and prepare the food.
- Tell him he has to choose two vegetables to go with supper – even if he's not going to eat them himself.
- Try to find a good role model. If you know of a child who eats up their greens, invite them to tea and lavish praise on their eating habits in front of your child.
- Keep the dessert well out of sight until the main course is finished.
- Don't give too much attention to your child when he says he won't eat something. Instead, reinforce the positive by commenting when he does eat the right foods.

Try making fruit and vegetable juice cocktails by blending ready-made carrot or mixed-veg juice with your child's favourite fruit – see IDEA 16, *Get fruity*, for some inspiration.

Try another idea…

'I do not like broccoli. And I haven't liked it since I was a little kid and my mother made me eat it. I am President of the United States, and I'm not going to eat any more broccoli.'
GEORGE BUSH Senior, Forty-first President of the USA

Defining idea…

And if all the previous advice fails? Resort to stealth tactics. Hide those veggies in casseroles, stews and pasta sauces by puréeing a handful or two of steamed veg and simply stirring it in to your child's favourite food.

How did it go?

Q   My daughter is only interested chocolate at the moment. There's no way she will eat anything green.

A   *Try making this chocolate courgette cake with her, then. It may not be the healthiest way to encourage her to eat her greens – but hey, it's a start!*
    Line a 20×35cm baking tray with baking paper and preheat the oven to 190°C/350°F/Gas5. Beat together 125g/4½ oz softened butter, 125ml/4½ fl oz sunflower oil, 1 tsp vanilla extract, 200g/7oz soft brown sugar and 100g/3½ oz caster sugar until fluffy. Gradually add three eggs, beating well after each one, and then 125ml/4½ fl oz milk until mixed thoroughly. Fold 350g/12oz plain flour, 2 tsp baking powder and 4 tbsps cocoa into the mixture. Stir in 450g/1lb peeled and grated courgettes and pour the mixture into the tin. Bake for 35–45 minutes until cooked through. Leave to cool in the tin.

Q   My son will only eat potato. It's driving me crazy!

A   *Most children love potatoes in all their guises, so try mixing other puréed vegetables into mashed potatoes – swede works well, as does carrot, sweet potato and parsnips. Pour a tomato and vegetable sauce over a baked spud or roast root vegetable batons in the oven with a little oil to make alternative 'chips'.*

10

Cup winners

The drinks you give your child can have a real effect on her health.

So what should your child be drinking at six months, a year — and beyond? The answers are all here.

The Department of Health currently recommends that babies should be fed nothing but breast milk or infant formula, up until the age of six months, after which solids and other fluids can start to be introduced into the diet.

Parents are then advised to ensure that breast or formula milk and boiled cooled water make up the majority of drinks for babies up to twelve months old. Any other drinks, such as fruit juice drinks, should be highly diluted and limited to meal times.

WATER

If your baby is thirsty between milk feeds offer plain, boiled and cooled tap water up until the age of six months. After that, water can be taken straight from the mains supply.

If you wish to use a filter, follow the manufacturer's instructions and keep filtered water in the fridge, as the filtering process removes some of the additives, such as chlorine, used to keep tap water fresh (you will still need to boil and cool the water for babies under six months).

FRUIT JUICE

If your baby is over six months, occasional drinks of 100% fruit juices diluted with water, can be a good source of vitamin C. But be warned – fruit juice contains natural sugars and acids that can cause tooth decay. Too much juice can also adversely affect your child's appetite for milk and food, leading to malnourishment if you're not careful – so when and how you give it to infants and toddlers is important.

Fruit juice needs to be diluted one part juice to ten parts water. It's best to give it with, or just after, meals – when the protective saliva in your baby's mouth will help restrict tooth erosion.

Here's an idea for you... **To protect teeth, dental experts advise you to encourage your baby to drink from a cup as soon as he can hold one. They also suggest you discourage bottle feeding by the age of one year. For an easy transition, give your child a beaker to play with early on so he can get used to handling it.**

Never give juice in a bottle, as the slow sucking will bathe your baby's teeth in sugar for long periods. Babies and toddlers should only drink juice out of a spouted or ordinary cup.

BABY JUICE DRINKS

Fruit and herbal baby drinks contain restricted levels of sugar – however, like fruit juice, parents are advised to avoid them as much as possible to protect teeth and stave off a sweet tooth later on. If you want to offer them now and again, follow the dilution instructions carefully and apply the same rules as for 100%

fruit juice – always with or after meals and from a beaker only.

Confused about how much milk your child needs? Turn to IDEA 7, *The white stuff.*

Try another idea…

MILKSHAKES AND SMOOTHIES

Cows' milk should not be given as a drink to children under one year of age. Once your child is over twelve months and adept enough to handle a plastic cup, however, she may enjoy home-made milkshakes and smoothies.

More of a meal than a drink – blend soft fruit, such as banana, strawberries or mango, with milk or yoghurt until smooth. Avoid using flavoured milkshake powders or syrups, as many are high in sugar and additives.

Smoothies and milkshakes are an ideal way of encouraging children of all ages to eat fruit, and both drinks make a healthy and nutritious breakfast for a child who is reluctant to eat first thing.

SQUASHES, FIZZY DRINKS, SHOP-BOUGHT FLAVOURED MILK AND JUICE 'DRINKS'

These types of drinks are not suitable for young babies and toddlers. Drinks aimed at older children and adults often contain artificial additives such as sweeteners and colourings which are unsuitable for very young children.

Be particularly wary of anything labelled as a juice or fruit 'drink'. Many boast that they contain real fruit, added vitamin C etc., but most juice drinks contain less than 10% real juice and in some cases up to fourteen teaspoons of

'Water is the only drink for a wise man.'
HENRY DAVID THOREAU, American poet and philosopher (1817–1862)

Defining idea…

41

sugar. Those that claim to have no added sugar may very well contain artificial sweeteners – so always check the labels carefully.

If you want to give these types of drinks to older children, restrict them to meal times only so that their teeth will have a degree of protection from the sugar and acid content. Making rules about when these types of drinks can be consumed will also help to keep their consumption within healthy limits. Research shows that children who have lots of sugary drinks are more likely to be overweight than those that don't. Water or milk between meals is a better choice.

How did it go?

Q   We're going on holiday and I'm worried about the quality of the local water. Is bottled water OK for my baby to drink?

A   *Be very careful with bottled waters – some can be very high in sodium (salt). Some bottled waters such as Evian and Volvic, however, are suitable for babies: www.naturalmineralwater.org (The Natural Mineral Water Information Service) has a list of low sodium mineral waters which are suitable for babies and young children. Remember that bottled water is not sterile, so you still need to boil and cool it before giving it to your baby if he's under six months old.*

Q   Are no-sugar diet drinks OK for children?

A   *Whilst they may be low in sugar, diet drinks tend to be high in artificial additives – which is never a good thing. Anything containing artificial sweeteners should not be given to children under 3 years old. I would try and encourage your child to develop a taste for more natural drinks.*

11

Fussy eaters

It can be notoriously difficult to get toddlers and young children to eat what you want them to eat – when you want them to eat it.

Follow these cunning tips for foiling fussy eaters, however, and meal times needn't be a battleground.

So your little angel refuses breakfast? Or perhaps he will eat nothing but jam sandwiches. Don't despair. As long as your child seems to be a reasonable weight and healthy, you probably don't have too much to worry about. In fact, a recent report from the Royal College of Psychiatrists found over a third of under-5s are picky eaters – and the habit, in their words, 'is a normal and common stage of development'.

Fussy eating at this age is thought to be a product of two things – a natural and healthy wariness of all the new textures and tastes your child is being asked to try, and a desire to test your reactions to his behaviour. To make sure your child gets through this phase as quickly as possible and with the minimum of upset, what's needed is some cunning nutrition know-how and the poise and patience of a poker player.

Here's an idea for you... **Involving your child in food shopping and meal preparation, will encourage a healthy appetite. Ask her to fill a bag with the best-looking apples she can find at the supermarket for example, or ask her to choose a piece of fish from the fish counter (even if it's 'for daddy' initially). Get her to help you chop the veg with a plastic knife, measure out some rice or lay the table. A little enthusiasm for good, healthy food will go a long way.**

The first and most common mistake most of us make is to unintentionally ruin a fussy child's appetite by giving him too many snacks throughout the day. If your child is eating very little at meal times it's natural to want to try and compensate with snacks. Unfortunately this usually only serves to fill him up – making the chance of his eating a proper meal later in the day much more unlikely. Give your child the opportunity to get hungry however – by limiting snacks to fruit and plain water and ensuring he gets plenty of fresh air and exercise between meals – you will be amazed at what he can and will eat.

The way you present a meal is also vitally important right now if you want your child to eat well:

- Make an effort to sit down and eat with your child at meal times, even if you're going to have your supper later. Having a drink or piece of fruit with your child whilst he eats will encourage him to relax and enjoy his meal.
- Keep portions small. A huge pile of food can seem overwhelming to a small child.
- Introduce new foods without comment. A quip about giving your child something he hasn't tried before or it being 'good for him' will often be enough to get him to refuse before he's even tried it.

- Choosing child-friendly versions of foods will make him more likely to eat them (but again, don't present them with an enormous flourish – or you stand to be rebuffed). Animal shaped pasta, mini sausages and sandwiches cut into interesting shapes with cute cookie cutters may sound a bit *Desperate Housewives* – but serve them up with your child's 'special' bowls and cutlery and you might just get a clean plate.

- When your child leaves something on his plate saying that he doesn't like it, take the offending food away without comment – but don't give up. Try it again a couple of days later – perhaps served in a different way. Experts reckon you should expect to offer an unfamiliar food at least eight to ten times before a child will accept it.

- The best way to broaden your child's appetite is to introduce just one new food at a time – and always alongside old favourites. Stir some tuna into his pasta with tomato sauce, for example, or add a little chopped spinach to a home-made chicken nuggets recipe or Bolognese sauce. But whatever you do, don't mention the new food – before or after he's eaten it.

Check your child isn't filling up on drinks. What she drinks and when can have a huge effect on her appetite. Go to IDEA 10, *Cup winners*, for the best advice.

Try another idea…

'Ask your child what he wants for dinner only if he's buying.'
FRAN LEBOWITZ, American journalist

Defining idea…

45

How did it go?

Q   **I've tried all your advice – but my three-year-old daughter still refuses to eat very much at all at meal times. She's got a great appetite for snacks like crisps and chocolate biscuits though. Surely any food is better than nothing at this age?**

A   *It is SO tempting to give a child a biscuit, bar of chocolate or crisps when you know that she's had nothing to eat – but you must stand your ground while you still have some control over what she's eating. If she knows she's going to get a chocolate biscuit when she doesn't eat her lunch, she's going to turn down her main meal every time. Don't encourage her taste for overly sweet or salty foods as it is likely to turn into a habit that will be much harder to break later on. Stick to your guns and offer healthy snacks like a banana or wholewheat toast with peanut butter when you really need to.*

Q   **But she only likes biscuits and Cheesy Do-Dahs – she won't eat fruit or toast with peanut butter. I'm scared she'll starve ... what shall I do?**

A   *Believe me, she'll eat what you give her if she's hungry – and you keep your nerve.*

12

Label conscious

Discovering some of the food manufacturers' more cunning labelling tricks will help you to make the very best food choices for your family.

Labelling on food and drink packaging can be very misleading, and many of the 'healthy' eating claims can be hard to trust. Here, some of the more common packaging claims are debunked.

1   VITAMINS AND MINERALS

Manufacturers love to boast how many vitamins and minerals their products contain – but this can be a smokescreen for their products' less desirable ingredients.

Whatever the product says on the front, always take a look at the nutrition box on the back. A 500ml blackcurrant drink that claims to be 'rich in vitamin C' can also contain a whopping 14 teaspoons of sugar – the equivalent of three and a half packs of chewy sweets. A pot of fromage frais that claims to be 'a source of calcium' may also contain a less-than-healthy four teaspoons of sugar.

'Added calcium' is another claim flashed across the packets of some children's processed cheese snacks. Added calcium there may be – but many of these snacks contain extremely high levels of salt – and a clutch of additives too if you ignore the claims and take a look at the nutrition box on the back.

2   IT'S 'REDUCED'

The term 'reduced' sugar, salt or fat can be confusing. To be able to claim a product has 'reduced' levels of anything means the food has to contain 25% less of the nutrient referred to than was in the original product. Unfortunately, if that particular product was very high in sugar, salt or fat in the first place – the 'reduced' version may still contain very high levels of sugar, salt or fat.

For example, some 'reduced fat' packets of crisps actually have more fat grams than other, regular packets of crisps – because their original version was particularly high in fat. Ditto a 'reduced sugar' soft drink may still have a high sugar content, because the sugar in the original was through the ceiling in the first place.

3   YOU SAY 'FLAVOUR' – I SAY 'FLAVOURED'

Here's an idea for you...

Keep an eye on fruit juice labelling. 'Pure' or 100% fruit juice is real fruit juice – a fruit juice 'drink' is not. A fruit juice drink, despite the apples, blackcurrants or strawberries crowding the label, may contain relatively little real juice and a lot of water, sugar and additives.

Flavour and flavoured – believe it or not, there is a big difference between these two terms when it comes to food labelling. A strawberry 'flavour' yogurt is one that has been made to taste like strawberries through the use of artificial flavours – it doesn't have to contain any fruit at all. A strawberry 'flavoured' yogurt on the other hand has to have most of its flavour coming from real strawberries.

4 'LIGHT' OR 'LITE'

These two terms can be used to refer to the
texture of a product as well as the amount
of fat it doesn't contain – there's no real legislation for these two terms as yet. So a
fluffy, high fat chocolate mousse could still be labelled as 'light'.

5 X% FAT FREE

X% fat free – although the food industry is supposed to have dropped this label,
many foods still advertise themselves as 97% fat free, 90% fat free and so on. If
you see something like a packet of biscuits or dessert labelled as 97% fat free don't
assume it will be better for your family, or lower in calories. Although it may contain
just 3% fat – it may be packed with sugar. Manufacturers often add sugar to replace
fat they've cut out. As always, have a look at
the label.

6 'HEALTHY' RANGES

Don't be complacent because a food belongs to
a supermarket's 'healthy' range. Some surveys
have discovered that in 'healthy' foods where
the fat content has been lowered – like cakes
and biscuits – the salt and sugar levels have been substantially increased. In ready
meals, the food may only be lower in fat because the amount of meat in the product
has been cut. Sugar or bulking agents may have been used to make up for the loss.
The same goes for children's 'healthy' foods. Additives may have been reduced, but
still take the time to check the labels for salt, sugar and saturated fat content.

To find out what 'organic'
labelling really means turn to
IDEA 25, *Plan-it organic.*

Try another idea…

'*We are living in a world today
where lemonade is made
from artificial flavours and
furniture polish is made from
real lemons.*'
ALFRED E. NEWMAN, *MAD* magazine
cartoon character

Defining idea…

49

Many 'healthy' wholegrain cereals specifically targeted at children and families contain high levels of salt and sugar too.

The good news is baby foods – foods and drinks made for children under the age of one – are heavily regulated. There are strict limits on additives and standards for nutritional quality that manufacturers have to abide by.

How did it go?

Q   This all sounds very complicated ... is there anything I can give my child to eat that I don't have to worry about?

A   *Obviously your very best bet is to cook at home, from scratch. That way you will know exactly what has gone into your child's meal. But that is hardly going to be practical all of the time. So if you care about your child's health, when it comes to processed foods and drinks you really do need to read the labels I'm afraid. Don't be seduced by the manufacturers claims on the front of the packet – turn the product over and read the nutrition box. There are simple guides to sugar (IDEA 22), salt (IDEA 21), fats (IDEA 26) and additives (IDEA 13) in this book that will make it easy for you to do so.*

Q   I can feel a headache coming on – it's so confusing – can you simplify it for me?

A   *I promise you, it really isn't too complicated. The best way to get a handle on label reading is to compare the nutrition boxes of two or three versions of the same food. That way you'll be able to see which one has the most salt, additives and so on. It won't take long to find the products you want to buy – and the ones you don't.*

13
E-asy does it

If you have concerns about additives in your child's food then this section will help to make what seems like a complex issue much simpler.

Knowing what's in your food is important and, honestly, you really don't need a degree in chemistry to find out.

So what exactly is an E number? Individual additives are given an E number to show that they have passed safety tests and have been approved for use here and in the rest of the European Union. EU legislation requires most additives used in foods to be labelled clearly in the list of ingredients, either by their name or by their E number.

BABY FOOD

The good thing in the UK is that any food, formula or drink aimed at children up to the age of twelve months falls under strict regulations about what it can and cannot contain. These rules cut down on the number of additives your baby can be exposed to and also set nutritional guidelines – including how much sugar and salt can be in a food, what the minimum amount of protein allowed is and how detailed a product's labelling needs to be.

CHILDREN'S FOOD

The bad news about foods aimed at children over a year old is that the legislation that protects babies suddenly doesn't apply any more. Although some additives are prohibited in foods marketed for children under 36 months – those types of foods are few and far between. Children aged one and over can basically eat absolutely anything. If you're buying processed food, it can contain high levels of sugar, salt, a broad range of additives – and the labelling can be a lot less comprehensive than it is on baby food. It's suddenly left to you to decide what food your child eats – and what additives are in it.

A survey into conventional processed children's foods undertaken by organic food company Baby Organix discovered that most foods contained an average of five additives (ingredients that you wouldn't add if you were making it yourself). The biggest culprits were children's desserts, cereal bars, breakfast cereals, children's drinks and frozen beef burgers.

Here's an idea for you... **Avoid bulking agents if you can. Modified starch, modified cornflour, maltodextrin and starch are all used to bulk out foods. Whilst they contain calories, they have very few nutrients. Growing children need plenty of good nutrients, not empty calories – so foods containing bulking agents are best avoided.**

Forewarned is forearmed, however. According to top nutritionist Amanda Ursell, author of *L is for Labels* (published by Hay House), the following additives are some of the ones you really need to be aware of and try to avoid. However, the best rule of thumb is, if you're concerned about E numbers and don't recognise many of the ingredients in the food you are thinking of buying, or the list sounds like something you had to revise for a chemistry exam, don't buy it.

COLOURINGS

Dyes are used in food more for the convenience of the manufacturer than the benefit of
the consumer. They are usually used to mask
poor quality ingredients and thereby mislead
the consumer as to the content of food.

**For more advice on reading
labels go to IDEA 12, *Label
conscious.***

*Try
another
idea...*

Azo dyes, found in many foods, are particularly controversial. Most azo dyes have
been given an E number by the EU – which means they are considered to be safe
to be used in the UK by the European Union. However the majority are banned
in many countries, including the USA, Japan and Scandinavia, as there is some
evidence that some can trigger asthma, skin rashes, rhinitis (a runny nose) and
may even be responsible for hyperactivity in some children, although this is hotly
contended by many manufacturers. If you think that additives may be contributing
to your child's health or behaviour in a negative way – go with your instinct and try
and avoid the following (the E numbers for food colourings run from E100–E180):

- E102 Tartrazine
- E104 Quinoline yellow
- E110 Sunset Yellow
- E122 Carmoisine
- E123 Amaranth
- E124 Ponceau 4R
- E128 Red G
- E155 Brown HT

*'Fake food – I mean those
patented substances
chemically flavoured and
mechanically bulked out to
kill the appetite and deceive
the gut – is unnatural, almost
immoral, a bane to good
eating and good cooking.'*
JULIA CHILD, cookery writer
(1912–2004)

*Defining
idea...*

PRESERVATIVES

Found in processed foods, preservatives are there to prolong shelf life. The ben-
zoates, sulphites, nitrates and nitrites are particularly well known for triggering side
effects for some children with asthma. Skin rashes and gastrointestinal problems
can also be linked to some preservatives (E numbers for preservatives run from
E200 to E285). In the Baby Organix study, the foods found to have the highest levels
of preservatives were burgers, sweets and children's drinks. Here are some to avoid:

- E210 Benzoic acid
- E211 Sodium benzoate
- E212 Potassium benzoate
- E213 Calcium benzoate
- E214 Ethyl p-hydroxybenzoate
- E215 Sodium ethyl p-hydroxybenzoate
- E217 Sodium propyl p-hydroxybenzoate
- E216 Propyl p-hydroxybenzoate
- E218 Methyl p-hydroxybenzoate
- E219 Sodium methyl p-hydroxybenzoate
- E220 Sulphur dioxide
- E221 Sodium sulphite
- E222 Sodium hydrogen sulphite
- E223 Sodium metabisulphite
- E226 Calcium sulphite
- E227 Calcium hydrogen sulphite
- E230 Biphenyl
- E231 Orthophenyl phenol
- E232 Sodium orthophenyl phenol

- E239 Hexamethylene tetramine
- E249 Potassium nitrite
- E250 Sodium nitrite
- E251 Sodium nitrate
- E252 Potassium nitrate.

Q   **A lot of foods have 'flavourings' listed on their labelling. Should I be concerned about such a vague ingredient?**

How did it go?

A   *Yes. Unfortunately there are fewer controls over flavourings and flavour enhancers than in most other areas of food manufacture – not least when it comes to labelling. The word 'flavouring' can be used to cover over 4,000 different chemicals. Of most concern is the widespread use of flavour enhancers such as monosodium glutamate (MSG), guanosine and sodium 5-ribonucleotide, because these chemicals can cause an adverse reaction in some children. These particular flavourings tend to turn up a lot in savoury snacks.*

Q   **Any advice on avoiding additives without having to read labels all the time?**

A   *Choose natural, unprocessed foods as often as possible. When buying con-venience foods choose canned or frozen basics to cut down on the number of preservatives that are likely to have been used – and finally, try to do more home cooking.*

14

Snack attack

Almost a quarter of most children's daily energy intake comes from nibbling between meals. So it's important you offer them healthy choices.

Without doubt, snacking is a major pastime for most kids, and the following will help you to distinguish between the good and the bad.

Snacking itself isn't necessarily a bad thing. Young children frequently need one or two snacks a day, as their stomachs are so small they simply can't get all the nutrients and calories they need through meals alone. For children of all ages, the right snacks can also help to keep blood sugar and energy levels up and can even improve their concentration levels throughout the day.

It's the content of your child's snack that makes all the difference, however. Prepackaged snack foods such as crisps, biscuits, processed cheese and cakes tend to be high in calories, salt, sugar and additives – and low in nutrients. These fattening, energy sapping foods are best avoided.

Until your child reaches her teens, the majority of her snacks will be bought by you – so do try to stick only to the foods you really want your child to eat. And set a good example yourself. You can't expect your child to settle with fruit slices and water if you're hoovering up handfuls of crisps and washing them down with cola.

Here's an idea for you...

Kids will enjoy making their own snacks

- Children of four years and over will enjoy helping to make popcorn – a healthy alternative to crisps. Popcorn is unsuitable for children under four because it is quite easy for little ones to choke on.
- Children of all ages will love a home-made fresh fruit lolly on a hot summer day. Buy a set of lolly moulds and let your child fill them with a fruit purée or yogurt and fruit smoothie, then leave them in the freezer until they set.
- Teenagers can make up their own dried fruit and nut mixes. Let them choose their favourite ingredients and throw in a handful of chocolate chips.

One of the keys to healthy snacking is to ensure you don't get caught on the hop, particularly when your child announces she's hungry and you're standing right next to the sweet and crisp section in the newsagents.

A couple of boxes of raisins, small bags of dried fruit, breadsticks, rice cakes, oat cakes and small cartons of long-life organic fruit juice are all ideal emergency supplies that will keep for weeks in a car glove box, child's backpack or handbag.

If you're organised enough to take fresh foods out with you on trips – and organised enough to remember to take the leftovers out of your bag when you get home (anyone who has removed a two-week-old banana from the corner of their handbag will know what I mean) – then it's a great idea. Small-cut peanut butter or Marmite sandwiches do pretty well for half a day or so in an airtight container. Ham, chicken, cheese, fish or egg sandwiches are not suitable unless you want to carry them in a cool bag. Slices of fruit bread and malt loaf are handy sweet alternatives that can be wrapped in foil or cling film and carried about all day.

Small, firm apples travel quite well, as do clementines, which are best peeled, segmented and stored in pot, so you don't have to wander round with a pocket full of peel looking for a bin. Berries and grapes are easy to eat on the move too. Slice grapes and strawberries for children under five as they are easy to choke on. The Banana Guard solves the problem of bruised and battered fruit. A handy plastic case that fits most bananas, it also gives you somewhere to store that smelly, sticky skin until you get home. Available in nine funky colours (including glow-in-the-dark) log on to www.bananaguards.co.uk or call 01473 211138 to order.

If your child has refused breakfast, or only eaten a tiny lunch, you will probably need to provide a more substantial snack that will fill a hole but won't spoil her appetite for the next meal. Good suggestions are:

- a slice of cheese on toast;
- vegetable crudités with hummus;
- fromage frais with berries or fruit purée;
- an oatcake and a slice of cheese;
- a bowl of soup;
- a fruit and yogurt smoothie;
- a crumpet with low sugar jam; or
- a hot cross bun.

Try another idea…

The kinds of drinks you offer your child throughout the day can make a dramatic difference to his health too. Read IDEA 10, *Cup winners*, for advice.

Defining idea…

'It's a very odd thing –
As odd as can be –
That whatever Miss T. eats
Turns into Miss T.'
WALTER DE LA MARE (1873–1956),
British poet

How did it go?

Q   I don't think my kids will see plain popcorn as a credible alternative to crisps somehow. Any other suggestions?

A   *If plain popcorn is 'boring' – give it some flavour. Once the corn has popped, melt a knob of butter, a tablespoon of honey and ½ teaspoon cinnamon together, pour over the popcorn and mix well. Alternatively melt a knob of butter, a tablespoon of muscovado sugar and ½ tablespoon cocoa together and do the same. For a savoury version toss the corn with a knob of melted butter mixed with a generous pinch of cayenne pepper.*

Q   Is there such a thing as a healthy biscuit?

A   *Not really. Many biscuits that are advertised as being low in fat are often higher in calories than regular biscuits. The manufacturers add more sugar to make up for the change in taste and texture. Regular biscuits with a high fruit content like fig rolls and garibaldi are lower in calories and fat grams than most. Jaffa cakes have just 1g fat and 45 kcals per biscuit – but they are packed with sugar and chocolate. Biscuits, like any other food, are fine in moderation – just limit the number you offer and don't let your child have them every day.*

15

Back to school

Your child is off to infant school and becoming much more independent. What should he be eating?

With activity packed days and rapid growth spurts, a varied diet containing adequate energy and nutrients is essential for normal growth and development now.

Unless he has a food allergy or health problems, once your child reaches five years old, the guidelines for his diet are more or less similar to that of an adult.

So what does a child of primary school age need to eat to have a balanced diet? The following list is based on the widely accepted Food Pyramid, and guidelines laid down by the American Academy of Paediatrics. It gives you some idea of the amounts of foods from the various food groups that your child should be eating every day. A cup is the US measurement of 225ml – roughly half a small mugful.

For all-day energy, encourage your child to have three main meals a day and two or three small snacks.

You do not have to stick to these daily recommendations rigidly, as long as your child's diet is pretty well balanced over the period of a week or two. If your child falls into the 7–10 years old category, use his age, appetite and the amount of activity he gets to guide you on the number of portions of each food he should be eating.

To find a fun, personal food pyramid, tailored to your child's age and lifestyle – and lots of helpful dietary tips – log on to www.MyPyramid.gov.

Here's an idea for you...

When it comes to your child's health, regular exercise is just as important as a balanced diet. It is recommended that children and young people have at least 60 minutes of exercise every day; and also that activities that increase muscle strength, flexibility and improve bone strength, such as swimming, cycling, sports and dancing, should be included at least twice a week.

5–6 YEARS OLD

- Starchy carbohydrates (bread, potatoes, rice, pasta, breakfast cereals). Recommended daily servings: 6.
  One serving is: ½ a slice of bread *or* ⅓ cup of cooked rice or pasta *or* ½ cup breakfast cereal *or* two small pieces boiled potato *or* ½ medium jacket potato.
- Fruit. Recommended daily servings: 2.
  One serving is: ½ an average pear, apple or orange *or* ¼ cup tinned or cooked fruit *or* ⅓ cup 100% fruit juice.
- Vegetables. Recommended daily servings: 3.
  One serving is: ¼ cup cooked vegetables *or* ½ cup salad.
- Dairy (milk, cheese, yogurts, fromage frais etc.). Recommended daily servings: 2.
  One serving is: ½ cup of milk *or* a small pot of yogurt *or* a matchbox-sized piece of cheese.
- Meat, poultry, fish, eggs, pulses, nuts and seeds. Recommended daily servings: 2.
  One serving is: 30g of meat, fish or poultry *or* one egg *or* ⅓ cup cooked pulses *or* 20g nuts.
- Fats and sweets. These should be kept to an absolute minimum.

7–10 YEARS OLD

If you're worried about your child's weight turn to IDEA 24, *Weighty issues.*

Try another idea...

- Starchy carbohydrates (bread, potatoes, rice, pasta, breakfast cereals). Recommended daily servings: 6–11.
  One serving is: 1 slice bread *or* ½ cup cooked rice *or* pasta *or* ⅔ cup breakfast cereal *or* 3 small pieces boiled potato *or* 1 medium jacket potato.
- Fruit. Recommended daily servings: 3–5.
  One serving is: 1 piece fresh fruit *or* ⅓ cup tinned or cooked fruit *or* ½ cup 100% fruit juice.
- Vegetables. Recommended daily servings: 3–5.
  One serving is: ½ a cup of cooked vegetables *or* a full cup of salad.
- Dairy (milk, cheese, yogurts, fromage frais etc.). Recommended daily servings: 2–3.
  One serving is: a full cup of milk *or* 1½ pots of yogurt *or* a matchbox-sized piece of cheese.
- Meat, poultry, fish, eggs, pulses, nuts and seeds. Recommended daily serving: 2–3.
  One serving is: 60–90g meat, poultry or fish *or* 1–2 eggs *or* ½ a cup cooked pulses *or* 30g nuts.
- Fats, sweets and salt. Fatty, sugary and salty foods should be kept to a minimum.

The amount of fat required by children drops slightly once they reach five years of age. Aim for fat to make up no more than 30–35% of your child's total daily calorie intake now. Keep saturated fats to an absolute minimum by making sure red meat is lean, and creamy sauces and fat-packed snacks are

'I have never let my schooling interfere with my education.'
MARK TWAIN, author (1835–1910)

Defining idea...

63

avoided as much as possible. You should also boil, poach or steam foods rather than fry them.

Junk food, ready meals and takeaways should feature rarely and sweets, biscuits, cakes and crisps should be an occasional treat rather than a daily must-have.

Watch what your child is drinking too – some juice drinks and fizzy beverages can contain as many as 14 teaspoons of sugar. Stick to water, diluted 100% fruit juice and milk. You can give semi-skimmed milk rather than whole milk now.

Choose and prepare foods with little or no salt too. For more detailed information on fats and sugary and salty foods read the relevant chapters in this book.

How did it go?

Q How can I be sure that my daughter is getting all the nutrients she needs?

A Ring the changes where family meals are concerned. Variety is very important. The more varied the food your child eats, the broader the selection of nutrients she will be getting. Although children tend to be creatures of habit, don't let her have the same breakfast cereal, sandwiches and snacks every day.

Q And you say I should limit the number of junk food snacks she eats? I'm finding it hard to stop her raiding the biscuit and crisp drawer now she's more independent. What can I do?

A Well, if you don't buy the stuff, your child can't eat it. Keep lots of healthy snacks around instead – she'll soon get used to the change.

16

Get fruity

If you're having trouble getting your little angel to eat enough fruit – there are several simple steps you can take to encourage her.

Children should ideally eat at least two portions of fruit a day, because they are packed with valuable nutrients and fibre.

Firstly, always buy the very best quality fruit you can afford. Look for organic – and with the exception of exotic, tropical fruit choose home-grown whenever possible. Shopping carefully really will make a huge difference where taste and texture is concerned.

Secondly – and this may sound obvious, but I'm going to mention it anyway – ensure that whatever fresh fruit you choose to give your child is well and truly ripe. A ripe, juicy pear is delicious – a hard, not-quite-ready-to-eat one could put your child off pears for years.

Thirdly, think about the way you serve fruit. Your child may not like great lumps of fruit with the skin on, but she may enjoy it stewed then poured over yogurt or ice-cream, puréed or frozen in a sorbet, peeled and cut up small in a fruit salad, added to savoury dishes, blended into a smoothie or baked.

And finally, don't stick to just two or three fruit favourites. Broaden your family's fruit repertoire for maximum nutritional benefits.

THE CHOICE IS YOURS

Before you plump for apples, grapes and bananas – *again* – think apricots, pineapple, pears, nectarines, galia, charentais and honeydew melons, peaches, clementines, oranges, lychees, even sweet ruby grapefruit. All will go down well with kids. Alternatively, take your pick from the following super fruits:

Here's an idea for you... **Take children to a local pick-your-own farm. Kids will really enjoy a Sunday afternoon spent picking – and, of course, eating – strawberries, raspberries or blackberries. Alternatively, get your child to grow his own fruit – even if you don't have a garden. Strawberries and tomatoes (yes, the latter are, of course, fruit) do really well in pots, window boxes and gro-bags and are easy to look after. You can buy starter plants very cheaply from all garden centres at the beginning of the summer.**

■ Berries. High in vitamin C and fibre – fresh, tinned-in-juice or frozen berries (think strawberries, raspberries, blackberries, blueberries) are delicious stirred into yogurt, served with ice cream, added to fruit salad or thrown into a fruit smoothie.

■ Mangoes. With one of the highest levels of antioxidant nutrients beta carotene and vitamin C – mango is delicious puréed or even baked in a pudding or pie. Make a mango 'hedgehog' by slicing a ripe fruit in half, removing the stone and scoring the flesh (being careful not to cut through to the skin with the point of a sharp knife) to create a chequerboard pattern. Now fold the mango inside out, so that the cubes stand up – still attached to the skin.

- Kiwi. With a higher vitamin C content than oranges, the tiny black seeds in kiwi also have a value – they're packed with omega-6 essential fatty acids. Cut your kiwis in half and eat with a spoon, like a boiled egg – or purée and freeze in lolly moulds to make 'frog spawn' on a stick.

To find out why buying organic fruit is a good thing read IDEA 25, *Plan-it organic.*

Try another idea…

- Plums and prunes. Prunes are a good source of blood-boosting iron, and both have good levels of fibre. Be careful to control the amount of prunes and plums your child eats, however (you'll find more advice on portion sizes in How Did It Go?, below) as both fruits have well known laxative properties.
- Watermelon. Ideal for making fruit punch and freezing for lollies and sorbets – super sweet watermelon is, again, high in antioxidants. It's also a rich source of potassium, which can help keep the body's fluid balance in good order. A watermelon pip-spitting contest is a disgusting, but fun way to encourage reluctant fruit eaters. Alternatively, pick out the pips, blend the flesh and drink as a smoothie or freeze the pulp in lolly moulds.
- Avocado. Yes, like tomatoes, avocado is classed as a fruit rather than a vegetable. One of the richest sources of vitamin E – which is needed for immunity and healthy skin – avocado also contains some folic acid and a range of B vitamins which are essential for metabolising food and energy production. Puréed avocado makes an excellent weaning food for babies – and tastes great, mashed on toast or mashed up with finely chopped onion and a little lime juice to make guacamole dip.

'An apple is an excellent thing – until you have tried a peach.'
GEORGE DU MAURIER (1834–1896), illustrator and novelist

Defining idea…

67

How did it go?

Q **You say it's a good idea for children to eat at least two portions of fruit a day – but I'm not really sure what constitutes a portion – particularly when it comes to my toddler.**

A *Nutritionists suggest you should think of a portion as a handful – using the hand of the child that is going to eat the fruit rather than your own to judge the size of his portion. For teenagers and adults, one apple, banana, pear or orange might count as one portion. For smaller children, a quarter or a half of these amounts might be more appropriate.*

Q **Does dried fruit count as a serving?**

A *Yes, dried fruit like raisins, prunes, dried apricots, apple rings, mango strips and so on does count towards the 'five a day' fruit and vegetable recommendation, although you can only count dried fruit as one portion – no matter how much, how many different types or how many times you eat it during the day.*

Q **Are dried, tinned and frozen fruit just as good for you as fresh?**

A *Dried, tinned-in-juice and frozen fruit are healthy additions to any diet. Believe it or not, canned and frozen fruit can even sometimes contain more folate and vitamin C than their fresh cousins, as the fruit tends to be preserved very quickly after harvest. Fresh fruit that has been stored, chilled and flown thousands of miles can lose a large proportion of its more volatile nutrients.*

17

Start right

A well-balanced breakfast can have a noticeable impact on your child's health, mood, ability to concentrate – and eating habits for the rest of the day.

So, no matter how rushed you are, it's vital you make sure there's time for a nutritious family breakfast.

The first meal of the day is considered to be the most important for a number of reasons. Eating the right foods at breakfast time will stabilise blood sugar levels, making it less likely that your child will crave a boost from sugary, high fat or processed foods later in the day. Some studies have also found strong links between eating breakfast and improved learning, a better ability to concentrate, less irritability, more energy, less likelihood of overeating during the rest of the day and a general feeling of well-being.

The foods to avoid at breakfast most of the time are the sugary and over processed ones. They may go down well with your child, but sugary foods tend to lead to cravings for yet more sugary, over processed foods by midmorning. So avoid foods like chocolate- or honey-coated and sugar-frosted cereals – or those that have been baked into clusters. Chocolate spread, croissants, muffins, breakfast and cereal bars and pastries are also all best left off the menu. Instead, try to ensure your child has a combination of slow-releasing carbohydrates and protein, which will help to keep him full and offer a steady supply of energy until lunchtime. In addition, aim to add a fruit or vegetable to the meal. Read through the following suggestions for inspiration:

■ *A wholegrain cereal* (with minimal added sugar and fat – compare labels to find the best) served with chopped banana and semi-skimmed milk (NB semi-skimmed milk should only be given to children of two and over, younger children should have full fat milk).

   A recent study at Harvard Medical School showed that people who eat wholegrain cereals every morning are less likely to be obese than those who skip breakfast altogether. In addition, they are half as likely to have blood sugar problems which can lead to type 2 diabetes to have high cholesterol – both are risk factors for heart disease.

■ *Unsweetened porridge* – do try the plain, 'instant' microwave version for speed – made with half semi-skimmed milk and half water. Don't be tempted to add sugar or honey to sweeten it – use finely chopped fresh or dried fruit such as chopped strawberries or raisins instead.

   Porridge has a low GI (glycaemic index) score which means it gives a slow, sustained release of energy – helping you to feel fuller for longer. Oats have also been shown to help lower blood cholesterol levels.

Here's an idea for you...

For older children, try a bacon sandwich. A study carried out at Reading University found that a bacon sandwich breakfast was one of the best for improving brain power. Choose unsmoked, lean bacon and trim away fatty rind before grilling or dry frying. Serve between wholegrain, granary or seeded bread with the very thinnest smear of butter or spread.

- *Wholegrain, multigrain, seeded or fruit toast* with low sugar peanut or other nut butter, reduced sugar jam, a thin spread of butter and Marmite (use Marmite sparingly as it is high in salt), mashed banana, cream cheese or ham slices. Serve with some fruit juice or fruit slices on the side.

  The breads recommended above are the best breakfast choice as they release energy more slowly than white bread. White is fine too, as long as you don't offer it every day.

- *Eggs* – scrambled, poached or boiled served with a toasted wholegrain muffin and cherry tomatoes. Using Omega 3-rich eggs, which are widely available from supermarkets, is a great way to boost your child's intake of this useful essential fatty acid. Important for a healthy heart and circulation – Omega 3 is also thought to help improve children's concentration and calm hyperactivity.

- *A pot of natural bio-yogurt with fruit and muesli stirred in.* If you add your own 'sweeteners' and other ingredients to natural yogurt, you know exactly what your child is getting. Tempt reluctant kids to eat by letting them choose their own additions and stir them in.

- *A slice of wholegrain toast* with low sugar, low salt baked beans and a glass of mixed apple and carrot juice.

  Baked beans can be counted as one of your child's five recommended daily portions of fruit and vegetables. Buying the low sugar, low salt variety really is worth the swap, as the ordinary versions can contain substantial levels of both ingredients.

For smoothie and milkshake ideas turn to IDEA 44, *Whizz it up.*

Try another idea…

'Our results suggest that breakfast may really be the most important meal of the day.'

DR MARK PEREIRA, research scientist at Harvard Medical School

Defining idea…

How did it go?

Q   Your suggestions sound great – in theory. However, no matter how hard I try, I can never get my daughter to eat breakfast before she goes to nursery. I end up giving her biscuits to eat in the car on the way there. What do you suggest?

A   *Is the morning a bit of a rush for you?*

Q   Yes … why do you ask?

A   *When it comes to young children and eating – and this can apply equally to teenagers – one of the most important ingredients is time. Get your daughter up at least an hour before you need to leave the house, so that she has 20 minutes or so to 'come round' before you serve breakfast. (Make sure you've found her clothes, bag etc. the night before – so you're not rushed and stressed.) Then sit her at the table so she can't be distracted, and serve her something really small – a large plate of food can be really off-putting first thing. I find a piece of toast cut into a couple of animal shapes with cookie or play dough cutters always goes down well, or a small tub of flavoured fromage frais. I always add a favourite chopped fruit on the side – and a drink, of course. Whilst doing this, I would also make sure that you let her know that you've run out of biscuits.*

18

Moveable feasts

If you've run out of lunch box ideas – or simply don't know where to start – this chapter will give you the inspiration you're looking for.

A well-balanced packed lunch will provide your child with all the energy and nutrients she needs to for a busy day at school or nursery.

Have you been making nothing but processed cheese sandwiches for the last few weeks? Do you always end up packing your little angel off to school with crisps and chocolate bars because you're worried she won't eat anything else? You are not alone.

According to a recent survey of children's lunch boxes, carried out by the Food Standards Agency, the contents of most packed lunches are way too high in saturated fats, sugar and/or salt. The same survey also showed that almost half of the lunch boxes examined did not contain fruit and that most of the lunches included heavily processed snacks, crisps, chocolate, biscuits and sugary fizzy drinks.

Whilst it's tempting to include junk food 'treats' in your child's lunch box – or hip, processed foods that have been heavily advertised on TV – don't. A meal that's poor in nutrients and high in salt, sugar and fat will sap your child's energy levels and mental alertness – and over time could even set the foundations for future health problems and obesity.

Here's an
idea for
you...

If you want to add a healthier sweet treat to your child's lunch, try making these banana and date muffins. Preheat the oven to 220C/400F/Gas 6. Line a twelve hole muffin tin with paper cases. Beat together 225g/8oz self raising flour, 1 tsp baking powder, 110g/4oz light muscovado sugar, 50g/2oz stoned, chopped dates, three mashed bananas, a large egg, 150ml/¼ pint skimmed milk and 4 tbsps sunflower oil. Pour into muffin cases and bake for 20–25 minutes until cooked

So if you're now at a loss as to what to give your child, don't worry – it really is quite simple to put together a healthy packed lunch. Here's how:

A healthy lunch box should contain the following four basic elements. Try to vary the contents from day to day to ensure she gets a broad spectrum of nutrients.

1   *A portion of protein* (e.g. meat, fish, egg, cheese, beans, lentils, soya products, nuts, seeds and Quorn). Fill sandwiches, wraps, pitta bread or rolls with good quality roast chicken, turkey, ham, tuna, salmon, nut butter, cheese or egg – or add meat, fish or tofu to a pasta or rice salad.

2   *Some complex carbohydrates.* Complex carbohydrates are foods that offer a slower release of energy than refined carbs like white bread, white pasta, biscuits and cakes. Make sandwiches with wholegrain, multigrain or pitta bread and choose wholemeal pasta and brown rice for salads if possible.

3   *A calcium-rich food.* Cheese, yogurt, yogurt drinks, fromage frais and milk are all good sources of calcium – the mineral essential for healthy bones and teeth. Stick to whole milk dairy products for children under five.

     If your child can't tolerate dairy foods, consider alternative sources of calcium such as calcium enriched orange juice and soya milk.

4   *At least one portion of fruit and/or vegetables*
    for fibre, vitamins and minerals.
        Fiddly-to-eat items will tend to get
    left, so fill a small pot or freezer bag with
    peeled clementine segments or fresh
    pineapple pieces, grapes, sliced strawber-
    ries, carrot and cucumber batons, dried apricots or raisins

**Dips are another good
lunch box option. Turn to
IDEA 39, *Little dippers*, for
suggestions.**

Try
another
idea...

AVOID

■ Ready-made cereal bars, muffins and flapjacks. They may sound healthy, but
   they're often high in sugar and fat and come in big portion sizes. Make your
   own smaller, healthier flapjacks or muffins instead, or choose fruit bread, fruit
   scones or malt loaf.
■ Savoury snack foods. Over-processed cheese and ham snacks and crisps are
   usually high in saturated fat and salt. Some savoury snack foods can contain a
   child's entire salt allowance in just one portion.
■ Fruit juice 'drinks' and fizzy pop. Anything that's labelled as a juice 'drink' is
   often little more than a fruit flavoured sugary drink – which, like fizzy pop may
   also contain artificial colourings and preservatives. Fruit juice that's made with
   100% fruit, diluted 50:50 with water, is a better option – otherwise plain water,
   low sugar flavoured water, milk or a fruit smoothie.

A healthy lunch box may sound boring – but it
doesn't have to be. Cut sandwiches into stars
or animal shapes, then wrap in brightly coloured sandwich bags, sealed with stickers. Buy
brightly coloured pots to store small quanti-

*'Ask not what you can do for
your country, ask what's for
lunch.'*
        ORSON WELLES, actor, director
                            (1915–1985)

Defining
idea...

ties of fruit or snacks – and think variety. If your child has a different fruit/sandwich filling/yogurt or drink most days, she won't crave over-processed, salty, sugary, ready-made snacks.

It's also important to keep food cool until it's ready to be eaten, so an insulated lunch bag is a good idea. If you're organised, make the lunch the night before and store it in the fridge so everything is thoroughly chilled by morning. Alternatively freeze a carton of juice and add it to the lunch bag just before your child leaves the house. It will keep sandwiches cool and be defrosted and ready to drink by lunch-time.

How did it go?

Q I feel like a real killjoy taking the crisps out of my son's lunch bag – especially when all his friends take crisps to school. Any suggestions?

A   *Well, let's be realistic – most foods are OK in moderation. If you really want to give him some crisps I suggest you just don't give him the whole bag. Decant a small portion into an airtight tub instead.*

Q It's the salt content I worry most about – are some crisps a better bet than others?

A   *Yes, I suggest you buy 'salt and shake' crisps, the type that come with a separate bag of salt – and discard the salt.*

19

Pick your own

Taking children out to visit local food producers, pick-your-own farms, or better still, helping them grow their own fruit and veg is a great way to encourage them to eat more healthily.

When you encourage your children to discover where their food comes from, how it's made and how it's grown, it can make a real difference to the way they perceive and enjoy it.

It's not just kids that are curious to know where their food comes from either – we all want to know exactly what we're buying and how it's produced these days. Local papers and your local council will usually have information on producers in your area that sell direct to the public, or log on to Big Barn at www.bigbarn.co.uk – a website that tells you where you can buy meat, game, fish, fruit and vegetables, cheese and dairy products, drink, bakers' products and even nursery plants direct from the people who produce them.

Here's an idea for you... **Take your child fishing for her tea. Many trout farms have a 'catch your own' section. Look in *Yellow Pages* or contact the British Trout Association www.britishtrout.co.uk (0131 472 4080) to find your nearest farm.**

You don't always need to have a garden to have fun growing your own food either. Mustard and cress, for example, can be grown on a window ledge – strawberries and tomatoes in a window box or hanging basket. Here's how:

CRESS

Great for impatient children, mustard and cress grows really fast from seed – which is available from any garden centre. Make the project more fun by growing the cress on top of a yogurt pot face, so it looks like hair.

To start, peel the wrapper off a yogurt pot (or paint it white) then decorate it with a face. Scrunch up some wet kitchen paper and push it into the pot – followed by a layer of damp cotton wool – leaving a 2cm gap between the top of the cotton wool and the rim of the pot. Sprinkle the mustard and cress seeds on the damp cotton wool and press down gently. Put the pot in a warm, sunny place and you should see the seeds start to grow in about seven days. Keep the cotton wool damp – adding a little more water if it starts to dry out. Once the cress has grown to the right length – give it a 'haircut' with a pair of scissors and add to salads or sandwiches.

STRAWBERRIES

Easy to grow – even if you don't have a garden. These small, trailing plants take up very little room and grow well in pots and hanging baskets.

Strawberry plants can be bought cheaply from garden centres and planted outside from late June and throughout the summer. They like a rich, well-drained soil, so give them plenty of compost or manure. If planting in a hanging basket or container, water well during the growing season and feed every ten days with a high potassium fertiliser like tomato feed between flowering and harvesting the fruit. Once the fruit has ripened, pick immediately and eat within two days, otherwise freeze or use to make into jam.

Whether home grown or pick-your-own, excess fruit and veg can usually be frozen. Go to IDEA 51, *The big freeze,* **for tips.**

Try another idea…

TOMATOES

A grow bag or window box, a warm, sunny spot, plenty of water and a bottle of liquid tomato feed is all you need to enjoy a surprisingly large crop of delicious tomatoes.

Once the risk of frost has passed, buy one or two tomato plants from your local garden centre. Super-sweet cherry tomatoes tend to be kids' favourites, so look for Sun Gold, Lilliput or Gardener's Delight varieties. Plant out in a grow bag or window box filled with organic compost.

Drive a strong stake into the soil next to each plant and tie the plant loosely to it with soft twine (check the twine and loosen and retie as the plant starts to grow up the stake). Water the plants thoroughly, then continue to feed and water as needed (check the instructions on your bottle of tomato feed). Do not allow the plants to dry out. Once the tiny fruits have

'There can be no other occupation like gardening in which, if you were to creep behind someone at their work, you would find them smiling.'
MIRABEL OSLER, author of *A Gentle Plea for Chaos: Reflections From An English Garden* (1989)

Defining idea…

started to appear, pinch out any side shoots between the leaves and stem. Within three months your tomatoes will be ready to pick. Pick when red and ready to eat – the tomatoes will keep in the fridge for up to a week.

How did it go?

Q   I love the idea of growing something we can eat – but it's winter and we want to get started now! What shall we do?

A   *Mushrooms are really easy to grow indoors, at home. Most garden centres sell kits that include everything you need to grow them – or you can buy a huge selection of kits online, from basic button mushrooms to more exotic varieties like Shiitake and bright pink Love mushrooms.*

Q   My older children will definitely enjoy growing something unusual. Any other suggestions?

A   *You'll have to wait until the summer – but nasturtiums are fun.*

Q   But they're flowers, aren't they?

A   *Yes, but both the leaves and flowers taste great in salads – a bit like rocket, in fact. Nasturtiums are easy to grow from seed and can be bought in pots in the summer. They're particularly good planted near tomatoes as they attract the bugs that eat the bugs that damage tomato plants – and they look good trailing from a hanging basket too.*

20

Use your loaf

So – brown, white, wholemeal, granary, multigrain, pitta or ciabatta – which bread is best for your child?

Believe it or not, there are over 200 different types of bread available in our shops at the moment.

The ultimate convenience food, bread is a good, nutritious source of complex carbohydrate and vitamins. Most breads contain about 10% protein, are low in sugar, but can vary widely in their fat content.

Which bread to choose? Each type has its own advantages, so the answer is probably to ring the changes frequently and enjoy the wide variety of choices on offer.

WHITE BREAD

Because white bread has had its bran and wheatgerm removed, it initially has a much lower vitamin content than wholemeal and granary. By law, it has to be fortified with B1, iron and calcium, however. This doesn't fully restore the B1 and iron levels lost, but the calcium is replaced at higher than original levels, so white bread has twice as much calcium as most other breads. If your child likes white, just go for the best quality.

Here's an idea for you...
Mass produced breads usually contain more additives than you might imagine, in the shape of bleaching agents, preservatives and colourings. To avoid these look for organic or traditionally made loaves – or have a go at making your own. A breadmaking machine is really easy to use – just throw the ingredients in and turn it on. Your child will enjoy experimenting with different ingredients to make his very own designer breads too.

GRANARY

Granary bread is made with brown flour containing malted wholegrains to give a nutty taste and better fibre content. One slice has around three-quarters the amount of fibre of wholemeal and an equal iron content.

WHOLEMEAL

Contains all parts of the milled wheat grain, including the husk. Slice for slice, wholemeal bread contains almost three times as much fibre, over three times as much zinc, and almost twice as much iron as white bread.

MULTIGRAIN

Has added seeds and wholegrains, which means it's more slowly digested than many other breads and has a lower glycaemic index, helping to keep energy levels up and satisfy hunger for longer. Top marks for fibre, it also provides more essential fatty acids than most other types of bread.

'BROWN' BREAD

Bread described as 'brown' on the packaging is not the same thing as wholemeal. Most commercial brown breads are made from a combination of white and brown flour which means their nutritional content falls somewhere between wholegrain and white bread.

Children suffering from coeliac disease or who have a wheat or gluten intolerance cannot eat normal bread. Some breads labelled 'rye' and 'oat' still contain a small percentage of wheat, so check the ingredients list on the packaging carefully. Gluten- and wheat-free breads are available from most health food shops.

You can do more with bread than just make sandwiches …

FLAVOURED BREADCRUMBS

Forget shop-bought chicken nuggets, fish cakes and fish fingers – use day-old bread to make flavoured breadcrumbs. Remove crusts and blitz bread in a food processor with lemon zest, sage and black pepper to taste or try adding parmesan and oregano. Keep flavoured crumbs in sealed bags in the freezer for up to a month, and use to coat fresh fish and meat, dipping first in flour, then beaten egg, then breadcrumbs.

Try another idea…

Bread can have a relatively high salt content. One slice might contain between 0.5g and 1g salt. To find out more turn to IDEA 21, *Pass the salt.*

Defining idea…

'Good bread is the most fundamentally satisfying of all foods; and good bread with fresh butter, the greatest of feasts.'

JAMES BEARD, American cookery writer (1903–1985)

PANZANELLA

This unusual Italian salad is a brilliant way to use up stale bread – get your child to tear up the bread and help with the chopping!

Break four thick slices of stale ciabatta or similar open-textured bread into bite-sized pieces. Place in a bowl with six ripe tomatoes cut into chunks, a small, finely chopped red onion, half a cucumber cut into pieces the same size as the tomato, two finely sliced sticks of celery, a dessertspoon of pesto, 5 tbsps olive oil and freshly ground black pepper. Stir well and leave for 30 minutes. Serve as a salad on its own or as a side dish to grilled fish or meat.

SUMMER PUDDING

A great English dessert, and a cunning way to get kids to eat berries. Out of season, try it with frozen berries.

Put 500g/1lb 2oz raspberries, 250g/9oz redcurrants and 110g/4oz blackcurrants in a saucepan with 200g/7oz caster sugar. Cook over a gentle heat for five minutes until juices start to run and sugar has dissolved. Line a pint pudding mould with two layers of cling film, leaving plenty hanging over the sides. Take 16 slices of good white bread, crusts removed and use all but one to line the sides of the pudding basin – slightly overlap each slice as you go. Spoon in the fruit and juice, place the last slice of bread on top, then cover with the cling film. Place a small saucer that fits inside the mould on top with a 3 or 4lb weight on top of that and leave in the fridge overnight. Turn out, remove clingfilm and serve with cream or creme fraiche.

Q **What about garlic bread, focaccia and so on – where do those types of bread fit in?**

How did it go?

A *Speciality breads make a welcome change from your regular loaf. Pittas and bagels are particularly handy for filling with good things. Some breads like focaccia, cheese-topped rolls, garlic bread, croissants and naan tend to be high in fat, however – so as always, keep an eye on the labels and use those types of bread occasionally.*

Q **So bread can be a bit unhealthy then?**

A *As with everything, the key is moderation. More than the type of bread you choose, however, it's what you put on it that you have to be careful about.*

85

21
Pass the salt

According to the Food Standards Authority, the majority of children these days are eating much more salt than is healthy. How to cut down without compromising taste.

So just how much salt can your children safely eat — and how do you keep their salt intake under control? Read on to find out.

Our bodies need a very small amount of salt to work properly. Eating too much salt can raise blood pressure. And people with high blood pressure who eat too much salt are three times more likely to develop heart disease or have a stroke than people with normal blood pressure. If your child has too much salt now, it may well affect his health in the future. It is also likely to give him a taste for salty food, which means he's more likely to continue eating too much salt when he grows up.

Baby food, by law, is not allowed to contain added salt, as babies need just the tiniest amounts – less than 1g a day until they are 6 months old, and no more than 1g a day from 7 to 12 months.

This need is easily met through breast milk and infant formula, so never, ever add salt to food you give to your baby. Never give your baby processed foods that aren't made specifically for babies – such as breakfast cereals, instant oats and pasta sauces

To cut down the amount of salt your family eats:

- Check the labels on processed foods so you can choose those with the least added salt or sodium.
- Don't add salt to your cooking.
- Don't put salt on the table.
- Cut down on salty snacks such as crisps and nuts, and heavily salted foods such as bacon, cheese, pickles and smoked fish.
- Choose tinned vegetables and pulses that say 'no added salt'.
- Cut down on sauces, especially soy sauce, because these are usually very high in salt.
- Ask for unsalted chips and fries in restaurants and burger bars.

– as they may contain levels of salt, which his kidneys will be just too immature to deal with. Also try and keep salty foods such as cheese, bacon and sausages to a minimum.

Even as your child gets older, is weaned and starts to eat family food – there is no need to add salt to his diet. If you're buying processed foods, even those aimed at children, it's always a good idea to check the information on the labels carefully so you can choose the product with the lowest level of salt possible.

Lots of people think they have a relatively low salt intake, especially if they don't add it to their family's food. But just because you don't shake salt onto food or add it to cooking doesn't mean you don't have a high intake. At least three-quarters (75%) of the salt we ingest comes from processed food, such as break-fast cereals, soups, sauces, biscuits and ready meals.

So how can you tell if a product is high or low in salt?

Salt is made up of sodium and chloride. And it's the sodium in salt that can be bad for your health. You will usually see sodium included in the nutrition information on food labels. Some products also say how much salt they contain.

Use herbs and spices in place of salt to give your food flavour. See IDEA 41, *On the rack*, for more information.

Try another idea...

Below are the recommended maximum amounts of salt children should have in a day, although it's better if they have even less than these amounts:

- 1 to 3 years – 2g a day (0.8g sodium)
- 4 to 6 years – 3g salt a day (1.2g sodium)
- 7 to 10 years – 5g a day (2g sodium)
- 11 and over – 6g a day (2.5g sodium)

A teaspoonful of salt weighs approximately 6g – so you can see the tiny amount your child really needs.

If you look at the nutrition information on a food label, there will usually be a figure for how much sodium is in 100g of the food. Sometimes, you will see information about a portion/serving too.

- 0.5g sodium or more per 100g is a LOT of sodium
- 0.1g sodium or less per 100g is a LITTLE sodium

This means if you serve up a 500g ready meal that contains 0.5g sodium per 100g, your child will be getting a whopping 2.5g sodium from the meal – more than any child under 11 should have in an entire day.

'Help you to salt, help you to sorrow.'

French proverb

Defining idea...

89

- If the amount of sodium is between 0.1g and 0.5g per 100g, this is a MODERATE amount of sodium.

Sometimes sodium is listed in milligrams (mg). This means you need to divide the milligrams by 1000 to work out the number of grams.

Try to avoid foods that contain 0.5g sodium or more per 100g. If you eat foods that are high in sodium, it can be very easy to have too much. Try instead, to choose foods that are lower in sodium when you can – or do more home cooking so that you know exactly what's in your family's food.

How did it go?

Q **Do I really have to read labels? Surely it's easy to tell which foods contain too much salt – they'll taste salty won't they?**

A *Not necessarily. Foods that are high in salt don't always taste very salty, often because they have lots of sugar in them too – some hot chocolate powders, biscuits and breakfast cereals for example. Also, your taste buds might be used to a high level of salt, so you may not notice the saltiness of some foods. I'm afraid you're going to have to look at the labels.*

Q **Another thing. We use sea salt at home – isn't that a bit healthier than table salt?**

A *Unfortunately, no. It doesn't matter how expensive salt is, where it is from, or whether it comes in grains, crystals or flakes – it still contains sodium. It's the sodium in salt that can cause problems.*

22

Sugar, sugar

Baby foods have strict guidelines that keep added sugar to a minimum – but once your child reaches 12 months, it's over to you to monitor the sweet stuff. How to control your child's sugar intake without becoming a complete spoilsport.

It's easier to cut back on excess sugar in your family's diet than you might think.

Sugars occur naturally in many foods such as fruit and milk – which is fine, we don't need to worry about those. The sugar that is of concern is added sugar, the stuff in fizzy drinks, sweets, biscuits, some breakfast cereals and jam.

WHAT'S WRONG WITH SUGARY FOODS?

Foods that contain a lot of added sugar tend to have quite a high calorie content and low levels of nutrients. Sugary foods also don't tend to fill children up – the rapid rise and dip in blood sugar that sugary foods can cause, means children will often want another sugary snack soon after having the first one. Sugary foods and drinks can also cause tooth decay, particularly if they are eaten or drunk between meals. This includes fruit juice and honey.

Try halving the sugar you use in your recipes. It works for most things except jam, meringues and ice cream.

CUTTING DOWN ON ADDED SUGAR

Whilst the odd bag of sweets will not do any harm – it's important to try and cut down on your family's everyday consumption of sugar.

- Have fewer sugary drinks and snacks. Don't keep them in the house if you can help it.
- Instead of fizzy drinks and juice drinks, go for water or unsweetened fruit juice (remember to dilute these 50:50 with water for children). If your child likes fizzy drinks then try diluting fruit juice with sparkling water.
- Instead of cakes or biscuits, try a currant bun, a slice of melon or some malt loaf.
- Do not add sugar to hot drinks or breakfast cereal.
- Rather than spreading jam, marmalade, syrup, treacle or honey on your toast, try peanut butter, reduced sugar jams, mashed banana, or low-fat cream cheese.
- Choose tins of fruit in juice rather than syrup.
- Choose low sugar breakfast cereals rather than those coated with chocolate, sugar or honey.
- Watch out for condiments and sugar packed sauces for meat and fish.
- Check food labels to help you pick the foods with less added sugar or go for the low-sugar version.

READING FOOD LABELS

Some foods that you might not expect to have sugar added to them can contain lots, for example some 'healthy' breakfast cereals and cereal bars. Other foods can be higher in added sugar than you might expect, such as tins of spaghetti or baked beans. The only way to really find out is to read the labels, which is easy when you know how.

Worried about additives in your child's food? Take a look at IDEA 13, *E-asy does it.* Try another idea...

When you are checking food labels, you can use the following as a guide to what is a lot and what is a little added sugar per 100g food.

Look for the 'Carbohydrates (of which sugars)' figure in the nutrition information panel on the label.

- 10g sugars or more per 100g is A LOT of sugar.
- 2g sugars or less per 100g is A LITTLE sugar.
- If the amount of sugars is between 2g and 10g per 100g, this is a moderate amount of sugar.

Sometimes, only the total carbohydrate figure is supplied. If this is the case, look for where 'sugar' appears on the ingredients list. The higher up the list it is, the more sugar the product contains. Be aware that sucrose, glucose, glucose syrup, golden syrup, maple syrup, treacle, invert sugar, hydrolysed starch, honey, dextrose and maltose are all added sugars. These figures can't tell you how much of the sugars come from milk or fruit and how much comes from added sugars.

But food manufacturers can be tricky. They know that people are reading labels to find out how much sugar is in the product. So they may mix in small amounts of many different types of sugar. That way, no single kind of sugar is the main ingredient by weight. Add them all up, however, and sugar outweighs anything else in the recipe.

HOW MUCH?

The amount of sugar in some common foods may surprise you:

'*Things sweet to taste prove in digestion sour.*'
WILLIAM SHAKESPEARE, *Richard II*

Defining idea...

- A serving of tomato ketchup – 1 teaspoon of sugar.
- A serving of sugary breakfast cereal – 4 teaspoons.
- Small pot of fruit yoghurt – 4 teaspoons.
- A glass of cola – 8 teaspoons.

How did it go?

Q You say fruit juice and honey can contribute to tooth decay. I thought naturally sweet foods wouldn't be such a problem?

A   *The sugars found naturally in whole fruit are less likely to cause tooth decay because the sugar is contained within the structure of the fruit. But, when fruit is juiced or blended, the sugar is released. Once released, these sugars can damage teeth, especially if fruit juice is drunk frequently. Fruit juice is still a healthy choice, and counts as one of the five portions of fruit and vegetables we should be having every day, but it is best to drink fruit juice at meal times. Honey is a kind of liquid sugar – so I'm afraid it affects teeth in the same way as other sugars.*

Q Is it OK for my child to have soft drinks that contain artificial sweeteners instead, then?

A   *Personally, I would avoid those too. Whilst they might not affect the teeth in the same way as sugar-sweetened drinks, some experts believe that food and drinks sweetened with artificial sweeteners such as aspartame, acesulfame-K and saccharine encourage a sweet tooth. Perhaps even more important, the long-term effects of consuming artificial sweeteners is as yet unknown. I'd stick to water, milk and diluted fruit juice.*

23

Big kids

How to encourage hungry teens to eat regular, nutritious meals.

The first thing to bear in mind is that the nutrient and energy needs of teenagers are higher than those of any other age group.

Growth and development are especially rapid now, so the need for energy and some nutrients is particularly high. This demand differs significantly between boys and girls. Boys need quite a bit more protein and energy at this age than girls, due to their greater growth spurt.

The adolescent growth spurt usually begins around the age of ten years in girls and twelve years in boys. Both sexes will grow an average of 23cm (around 9 inches) and put on 20–26kg (44–57lbs) weight in total as they go through puberty. Before adolescence, both girls and boys have an average of 15% body fat. During adolescence this increases to about 20% in girls and decreases to about 10% in boys.

Obviously junk, processed and very sugary, fatty or salty foods should be kept to an absolute minimum now. The best way for teenagers to obtain the energy and nutri-

Here's an idea for you...

Experts recommend that teenagers have at least 60 minutes of exercise a day – yet the teenage years are the time when many children give up exercise and sport. In spite of their general lethargy, surveys show that most adolescents would like to be fitter. Encourage your teenager to try some more unusual, sociable activities or sports that she thinks she might enjoy. Think ice-skating, dance classes, martial arts, mountain biking, surfing, fencing, rock climbing ...

ents they need is to eat a varied diet of three well-balanced, nutritious meals with healthy snacks in between.

Although your child may want to hang out and hoover up junk food with his friends, try to balance this by keeping the food you provide as healthy as possible.

Ideally, teenagers should be eating:

- At least five portions of fruit and veg a day.
- Carbohydrates (e.g. bread, pasta, rice, potatoes) with every meal.
- Several servings of milk and dairy products daily.
- One or two servings of protein (meat, fish, eggs, nuts and pulses) each day – including at least two portions of fish a week, one of which should be an oily fish.
- Small, limited amounts of fat, including butter, margarine, oils and cream, and fried foods including crisps and chips and small, limited amounts of sugary foods including cakes, biscuits, sweets, soft drinks and ice cream.

Healthy 'between meal' snacks include:

- Fruit of any kind – sliced, dried or tinned in juice.
- Cold lean meats in a wholegrain bread sandwich.

- Peanut butter on toast.
- Hummus or cream cheese dips with bread sticks, chopped vegetables or fruit.
- Milk shakes made with semi-skimmed milk or a fruit smoothie.
- A pot of yoghurt.
- A bowl of low sugar cereal.
- Home made snack mixes of dried fruits, nuts and seeds with a handful of chocolate chips, mini pretzels or mini marshmallows thrown in. Divide the mix into individual portions in resealable plastic bags.

Other important dietary habits to follow during adolescence include:

- Drinking at least eight glasses of fluid a day (avoid sugar-packed drinks as much as possible – choosing water, diluted fruit juice of milk-based drinks instead).
- Eating breakfast – it will provide essential nutrients and improve concentration in the mornings.

CALCIUM IS KEY

The rapid increase in bone mass now means that teenagers actually require more calcium than adults. Boys should aim for 1000mg calcium per day and girls 800mg. A well balanced diet that includes a pint of milk a day should give enough calcium to fulfil these requirements.

Try another idea...

If your teenager is vegetarian, it's important that her diet is balanced and includes all the necessary nutrients. Read IDEA 33, *Tofu ... or not tofu.*

Defining idea...

'*Children aren't happy without something to ignore, And that's what parents were created for.*'
OGDEN NASH, American poet

Other good sources of calcium include dairy products such as yogurt and cheese (low fat milk and dairy products contain at least as much calcium as whole milk and its products), calcium-fortified soya milk and white bread. Pulses, nuts, dried fruit and green vegetables, such as spring greens and broccoli also contain calcium, as does fish that is eaten with the bones, such as whitebait or canned sardines.

AVOID IRON DEFICIENCY

Adolescents have been shown to be at particular risk of iron deficiency. In one national survey of children aged 4–18, almost 50% of teenage girls were found to have a low intake of iron, as well as a significant proportion of boys. Rapid growth, coupled with poor dietary choices, can result in iron-deficiency or anaemia – which can lead to chronic fatigue, heart palpitations and affect academic performance. Teenage girls need to pay particular attention to iron in their diets as their iron stores are depleted each month following menstruation.

The main dietary source of iron is red meat, but there are lots of non-meat sources too, including fortified breakfast cereals, dried fruit, bread and green leafy vegetables. The body doesn't absorb iron quite as easily from non-meat sources, but you can enhance absorption by combining them with a vitamin C rich food like orange juice and dark green vegetables.

Q   All my 15 year old wants to eat is chips, chicken nuggets and cola *How did*
– it's driving me insane. What can I do? *it go?*

A   Your teenager is more likely to follow your example than do what you say,
so try to stick to serving and eating healthy food at home. Even if you don't
see results in the short term, your good habits will show through in the
end.

Q   But meal times have become a bit of a battleground – any other
suggestions?

A   Compromise. Give her chips as long as she has grilled fish and vegetables
with them. She can have home-made nuggets, rather than the over proc-
essed kind. Let her have what she likes to an extent but refuse to give her
more than one poor dietary choice at any meal.

24
Weighty issues

Worried your child may be overweight? Everything you need to know about this sensitive issue.

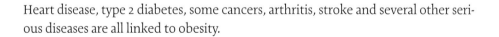

Children, quite naturally, come in all different shapes and sizes. But if your child is classed as clinically overweight, it puts her at an increased risk of becoming obese in the future and makes it much more likely she may develop a host of serious diseases.

Heart disease, type 2 diabetes, some cancers, arthritis, stroke and several other serious diseases are all linked to obesity.

HOW CAN I STOP MY CHILD BECOMING OVERWEIGHT?

If you are concerned about your child's weight – there are two issues that need to be addressed. The first is exercise. According to research, today's children eat fewer calories than their predecessors – but they're heavier because they're much more sedentary. Computer games, too much TV, driving your child everywhere and a lack of organised sport at school all need to be addressed if you want your child to be a healthy weight.

Here's an idea for you... **Keep an eye on portion sizes. The easy way to do this is to buy slightly smaller dinner plates (plates have actually steadily increased in size over the past few years).**

The second way to prevent your child piling on excess pounds is to make sure her calorie intake matches her calorie expenditure. The healthy eating suggestions in the chapter appropriate to your child's age in this book should give you a simple framework to work to.

In addition:

- Encourage your child to recognise when she is full – this may mean that you have to stop encouraging her to finish up everything on her plate.
- Look at the eating habits of the whole family – perhaps there are broader changes you need to make.
- Most important of all, remember that what you don't buy, your child can't eat. Healthy eating begins with the way you fill your shopping trolley.

Basically, if your child has a healthy, balanced diet – fatty and sugary snacks and drinks are kept to a minimum – and she gets plenty of daily exercise, she should maintain a healthy weight.

HOW CAN I TELL IF MY CHILD IS OVERWEIGHT?

You can get a good indication if your child is a reasonable weight for her height by working out her body mass index (BMI), then checking how her score measures up below.

To work out your child's BMI, you will need a calculator. First find her height in metres and then square it (e.g. $1.6 \times 1.6 = 2.56$). Now find her weight in kilograms (e.g. 45.5kg). Divide her weight by her height squared (e.g. 65kg divided by 2.56) and you have her BMI of 25.39. Now check her BMI against the recommended BMI for her age and sex. If the figure is higher than the one recommended, your child is likely to be overweight.

To find out more about fats in your child's diet read IDEA 26, *Get the right fat-itude.*

Try another idea...

The following BMI chart has been adapted from statistics put together by the Institute of Child Health and The International Obesity Task Force.

BMI chart - Your child may be overweight if he or she is

Age	Boys with BMI over	Girls with BMI over
2	18.4	18
3	17.9	17.6
4	17.6	17.3
5	17.4	17.1
6	17.6	17.3
7	17.9	17.8
8	18.4	18.3
9	19.1	19.1
10	19.8	19.9
11	20.6	20.7
12	21.2	21.7
13	21.9	22.6
14	22.6	23.3
15	23.3	23.9
16	23.9	24.4
17	24.5	24.7
18	25	25

WHAT TO DO IF YOU THINK YOUR CHILD IS OVERWEIGHT

If you have concerns about your child's weight – you must seek advice from your GP. Never put your child on a weight loss programme without seeking medical advice first. Your child's nutritional requirements will fluctuate with age – so don't be tempted to cut foods or groups of foods out of her diet unless you have been advised to do so by a doctor or registered dietician.

Around the onset of puberty girls and boys suddenly need many more calories to fuel the dramatic changes their bodies are going through. Girls start to deposit extra fat on their breasts, hips and thighs and boys become taller and more muscular. These developments are normal – so it's important they are not mistaken for weight problems.

EATING DISORDERS

Many children worry about their body image and size, so it's important you give your child plenty of encouragement and positive feedback – whatever her size. If your child is overweight, don't start to obsess about it. Eat meals together when you can and set a good example with your eating habits. Frequent weigh-ins, nagging and singling her out for special diet meals can just lead to more problems and may even encourage an eating disorder such as anorexia nervosa, bulimia or binge eating.

Defining idea...

'**Eat to live, and not live to eat.**'
BENJAMIN FRANKLIN (1706–1790)

If you are worried that your child may have developed an unhealthy relationship with food speak to your GP or contact the Eating Disorders Association – www.edauk. com – 0845 634 7650.

Q   My son loads up on fatty junk food and sweets at school. Any tips?

How did it go?

A   *First, make sure he has a healthy breakfast. Foods that give a slow, steady release of energy such as porridge, whole grain cereal, egg and/or beans on toast will improve concentration, lessen the craving for a sugary mid-morning snack and help to fill him up until lunchtime. Give him a packed lunch too – and only enough money for an emergency phone call. Surveys shows lunch and pocket money tends to get spent on sweets or junk food rather than in the canteen.*

Q   And how what about after school – he's always starving?

A   *Don't have crisps, sweets, sugary drinks and biscuits in the house. Keep plenty of fast, healthy snacks within easy reach instead. Think fruit bread, bananas, yogurts and yogurt drinks, toast and peanut butter, turkey sandwiches. Encourage your child to drink water or milk rather than sugary drinks too.*

25

Plan-it organic

Organic. The best food you can buy for your family – or just a big con?

The organic question is really difficult to cover as a single subject because it encompasses such a wide range of produce and issues — but here's a basic guide.

WHAT DOES 'ORGANIC' REALLY MEAN?

Organic farming methods are designed to produce food whilst maximising the health of the environment and of livestock on the farm. The use of artificial fertilisers, herbicides and pesticides are severely restricted and animals are reared without the routine use of drugs, antibiotics and wormers that are more common in intensive livestock farming. Genetically modified (GM) crops and ingredients are banned under organic standards. The result is produce that contains the absolute minimum of chemical residues and has a lower environmental impact than conventionally farmed foods.

To be able to call itself organic, a food or drink must have been certified organic by an independent body like the Soil Association. In the UK organic standards are rigorous. For a product to mention the word 'organic' in its name – e.g. Organic Beef Stew – at least 95% of its ingredients must be organic, and the label must tell you which ingredients are not. The non-organic ingredients can only be used because there are no organic versions of it.

ORGANIC BEST BUYS

If you're thinking of going organic, there are some products that are definitely worth making the change for.

Fruit and vegetables

Although conventional fruit and veg are regularly tested for pesticides, herbicides and fertiliser residues, if you're going to eat more of the stuff, it's probably best to opt for organic. This is particularly important in the case of fruit and vegetables that aren't going to be peeled before you eat them such as lettuce, celery and apples. Some pesticides used in conventional farming are designed to stay put in the rain, so are particularly difficult to wash off.

Here's an idea for you...

Just because something is certified as organic, doesn't mean it's super healthy. Some organic products, like breakfast cereals, cakes and biscuits, can actually have higher fat, salt and sugar contents than the non-organic versions. Sorry – but you've still got to read the labels!

Tests have shown that on average, organic fruit and veg contains higher levels of vitamin C, essential minerals and antioxidants than their conventional cousins too. However, some of these nutrients can be damaged by poor storage – so look for fresh produce that is stored in cool, non-bright conditions if you want to take advantage of those extra nutrients – don't just rely on the organic label.

Fruit squash

Colours, stabilisers and preservatives which have been linked to hyperactivity – and artificial sweeteners which may pose a particular risk to young children – can be found in some regular fruit drinking squashes but are not allowed in organic versions. This makes organic fruit squash a healthier option – but be warned, it's still high in sugar.

Dried fruit

As well as being produced from organic fruit, preserving ingredients such as sulphur dioxide and potassium sorbate are not allowed in organic dried fruit. Sulphur dioxide can cause wheezing in sensitive individuals.

Dairy produce

Recent research from Aberdeen University showed that organic milk can contain almost three quarters more of the essential fatty acid omega 3 than ordinary milk thanks to a higher proportion of clover forage in the diets of organic cows. Organic cheese is thought to contain even more Omega 3s than milk.

Wholemeal bread

Why buy organic? High-fibre bread is the most likely type of bread to contain pesticide residues because they can collect in the grain's

Organic poultry is definitely another good organic buy. To find out why turn to IDEA 29, *I feel like chicken tonight.*

Try another idea...

'High-tech tomatoes. Mysterious milk. Supersquash. Are we supposed to eat this stuff? Or is it going to eat us?'
ANNITA MANNING, American journalist

Defining idea...

109

outer layers – so buying organic does make sense. Just be aware that its lack of chemical preservatives may give organic bread a shorter shelf life.

Vegetable oil

Produced from organic crops, vegetable oil must be pressed, not solvent-extracted. Organic vegetable oils are not refined using high temperatures either.

If you are careful to keep organic vegetable oils in a cool and dark place to avoid oxidation, they may offer significantly enhanced health benefits. Fresh, unrefined oils contain essential fatty acids, oil-soluble vitamins and beneficial nutrients such as lecithin and plant sterols compared to their non-organic, refined cousins.

Chocolate, tea and coffee, bananas

Why buy organic? To prevent plantation workers being exposed to high levels of pesticides and other chemicals and to minimise the adverse environmental impact of conventional farming in poor countries.

Q   **I'd like us to eat more organic food – but it's so expensive! Why?**   *How did it go?*

A   *Organic foods are currently more expensive for a number of reasons. Firstly, the yields are on average between 10 and 20% lower than in conventional agriculture and, with some crops (potatoes, for example), it can be as much as 40% lower.*

   Also, production costs are higher. For example, organic farmers don't use herbicides so they have to weed some crops, such as onions and carrots, by hand. Such a labour intensive method contributes to a more expensive product.

Q   **Is it true that organic food tastes better?**

A   *Not always – it depends on where the food is from and how it's been stored. Buy an organic mango that has been flown half way round the world and you are unlikely to be able to tell the difference between it and a conventional fruit. Pop to your local farm shop for some just-picked organic tomatoes, however, and the slower, more traditional farming methods can make a world of difference to the taste. Try and source your organic food locally so it's super fresh if it's taste you're after.*

Q   **Is there somewhere I can go to find out even more about organic foods?**

A   *Yes. Try the Soil Association, the UK's leading campaigning and certification organisation for organic food and farming – www.soilassociation.org*

26
Get the right fat-itude

All children need some fat in their diets – but it has to be the right kind.

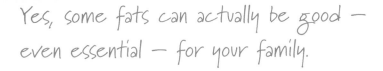
Yes, some fats can actually be good – even essential – for your family.

Up to the age of five, a child's diet should contain around 40% fat. After that, (although there were no set figures for children in the UK at the time of this book going to press), it is suggested that 35% of their calories should come from fat – although 30% is considered to be a better target by the World Health Organisation.

Whilst no child should be put on a low fat diet unless advised by a medical expert to do so, there is substantial evidence that reducing the amount of 'bad' saturated, trans and hydrogenated fats that we eat can lower our chances of developing coronary heart disease in later life.

Diets that are way too high in fat are also associated with obesity, which is currently reaching epidemic proportions in the UK. People who are obese are more likely to develop conditions such as heart disease, type 2 diabetes and some cancers.

So, as part of a general, healthy family diet we should all try to reduce the amount of foods we eat that contain hydrogenated or saturated fats and replace them with reasonable levels of healthy unsaturated fats. We should also be eating more long chain omega 3 fatty acids, which are found in oily fish.

THE FATS WE NEED TO EAT – AND THE FATS WE DON'T

Saturated fats

These are generally considered to be 'bad' fats. Solid at room temperature, they come mainly from animal sources. Think butter, lard, hard margarine, red meat, full fat milk and cheese. Coconut oil and palm oil are also high in saturated fat.

Eating too much saturated fat can increase the amount of cholesterol in the blood, which increases the chance of developing heart and circulatory disease.

Hydrogenated and trans fats

These are also considered to be 'bad' fats. Hydrogenation is one of the processes that can be used to turn liquid oil into solid fat. The final product of this process is called hydrogenated vegetable oil, or sometimes hydrogenated fat and it's used in some biscuits, cakes, pastry, margarine and other processed foods.

Here's an idea for you...

To keep an eye on how much fat your family is eating, compare the labels of different food products and choose those with less total fat and less saturated fat. Use the following as a guide:
- 20g fat or more per 100g is a LOT of fat
- 5g saturates or more per 100g is a LOT
- 3g fat or less per 100g is a LITTLE fat
- 1g saturates or less per 100g is a LITTLE fat
- If the amount of total fat is between 3g and 20g per 100g, this is a MODERATE amount of total fat. Between 1g and 5g of saturates is a MODERATE amount of saturated fat.

114

During the process of hydrogenation, trans fats may be formed. Trans fats raise 'bad' cholesterol and may be even more harmful than saturated fats. They have no known nutritional benefits.

For more information on oily fish turn to IDEA 34, *Fishing for compliments.*

Try another idea...

Unsaturated fats

Polyunsaturated fats and monounsaturated fats have been shown to lower blood cholesterol levels when eaten instead of saturated fat, and therefore help in reducing the risk of heart disease. Monounsaturates come mostly from vegetable sources. Think olive, rapeseed and groundnut oils, avocados and nuts. Polyunsaturates can be found in oily fish, seed, grain and nut oils.

TIPS FOR KEEPING FATS AT A HEALTHY LEVEL

- Choose lean cuts of meat and trim visible fat.
- Grill, bake, poach or steam rather than fry and roast.
- If you do choose something high in fat, such as sausages, pick something low fat to go with it – for example, boiled potatoes instead of chips.
- Compare food labels so you can pick the products with less total fat or less saturated fat.
- Swap fatty snacks for healthy ones most of the time – for example, vegetable sticks instead of crisps, a slice of wholemeal toast with peanut butter rather than cake or biscuits
- Put some extra vegetables, beans or lentils in your casseroles and stews and a bit less red meat.

'Life expectancy would grow by leaps and bounds if green vegetables smelled as good as bacon.'
DOUG LARSON, cartoonist

Defining idea...

- Measure oil for cooking with a spoon or use an oil spray rather than pouring it straight from a container.
- Don't use butter or spread in sandwiches if the filling is moist.

How did it go?

Q **There's so much publicity about the benefits of fish oils at the moment. Is it all hype?**

A *No, many experts now believe that the balance of Omega 6 (found in plant oils) and Omega 3 fatty acids in children's diets may be crucial for health. The bulk of children's polyunsaturated fat intake currently comes in the form of Omega 6s – so many experts believe it's the level of Omega 3s, found in oily fish like mackerel and salmon, that needs to be improved. Children who have taken part in trials of fish oil supplements appear to have better concentration, learning ability and behaviour – but more research is needed. Eating oily fish regularly can help to reduce the risk of coronary heart disease. Try to put oily fish on the menu once or a maximum of twice a week from the age of nine months.*

Q **If a food contains these scary-sounding trans fats, do they have to be mentioned in the ingredients and the nutritional information on the label?**

A *No. However, trans fats can be formed during the process of hydrogenation, which means that some foods that contain hydrogenated vegetable oil also contain trans fats. Hydrogenated vegetable oil must be declared in the ingredients list. If the ingredients list includes hydrogenated vegetable oil, there's likely to be trans fats in the product.*

27

Miracle meals

Seem to have run out of everything and don't have time to go to the supermarket? Reliable store cupboard staples that guarantee a huge choice of fast family meals.

Keep these versatile ingredients in stock
— and you'll be able to rustle up a nutritious family
meal in minutes.

The following larder, fridge and freezer staples may seem rather basic – but the good thing is, they'll never let you down

THE LARDER

Tinned pulses

Not just baked beans – but tins of mixed beans, cannellini beans, haricots, chick peas and butter beans (choose those with no added salt) are really handy for adding to stews, soups and salads.

- Stir cooked chopped bacon into mixed beans or add tuna to cannellini beans – warm either combination through and dress with a little garlic and olive oil before adding to cooked pasta shapes.

Here's an idea for you... **Couscous is a handy standby and really easy to make. Boil a selection of chopped mixed vegetables (tiny broccoli florets also work well) in a low salt bouillon for a minute or two until soft. Put some dry couscous in a bowl. Use a slotted spoon to add the vegetables, then pour over just enough boiling stock to cover the couscous. Mix vegetables, couscous and bouillon together, cover and leave for ten minutes. Stir in a little butter or olive oil and serve.**

■ Tinned beans can also be blitzed in a food blender with a little garlic, olive oil, lemon juice and herbs to make a nutritious home-made paté or hummus-style dip.

Canned tuna

Choose tuna canned in spring water rather than brine or oil. The small, individual portion tins are particularly handy for feeding young children in a flash.

■ Obviously, you can mix tuna with a little mayonnaise for a nutritious sandwich filling. Add finely chopped red pepper, red onion or sweetcorn to up the daily veg intake.

■ Stir a drained can of tuna into a plain tomato pasta sauce.

■ Use tuna to top jacket potatoes.

■ Scatter flaked tuna over salad leaves with sliced, still-warm, boiled new potatoes, cooked green beans and sliced boiled eggs (make a dressing with oil, vinegar and a little grain mustard) for a quick version of salad nicoise.

Tinned fruit in fruit juice

As a healthy snack, small ring-pull tins are also handy in packed lunches, as an instant dessert or breakfast cereal topper.

■ Drained tinned peaches and mango make excellent smoothies blended with yogurt.

Pesto

Kids seem to love pesto on anything.

For some more exotic ingredients that many children seem to like, check out IDEA 52, *Petits gourmets*.

Try another idea…

- Stir it into pasta.
- Add it, along with finely chopped roast vegetables or sundried tomatoes to cooked couscous.
- Mashed, baked or boiled potatoes love pesto.
- Spread it thinly on sandwiches in place of butter with fillings like roast chicken or mozzarella.
- Whisk a blob of pesto into oil and balsamic vinegar for a delicious salad dressing.

Pasta

Every parent's best friend.

- Serve it up in the conventional way with a sauce of your choice and parmesan, as macaroni cheese or lasagne.
- Add it par-boiled to soups or stews ten minutes before the end of cooking time to create a substantial one-pot meal.
- Cold pasta salads are handy for lunch boxes and snacks.

IN THE FRIDGE

Bacon

Bacon has a surprisingly long fridge life. Choose the best quality, least fatty version you can afford and keep it handy for grilled bacon sandwiches and cooked breakfasts, also:

- Use snipped, cooked bacon in pasta sauces, risottos and omelettes.
- A few finely snipped rashers of pancetta or smoked bacon really add depth to bolognese sauce.

Eggs

The ultimate fast food. Of course, there's boiled egg and soldiers, scrambled on toast, egg sandwiches, omelette or poached with beans – but also try:

- Cheese frittata – stir fry some finely cut veggies, (including onion and a little garlic) until soft. Then stir in two whisked eggs per person and a handful of grated cheese and allow to cook through until set. When nearly firm, sprinkle with a little more cheese and place under the grill until brown.

IN THE FREEZER

Frozen vegetables

Many frozen vegetables (and fruits) have higher levels of nutrients than much of the fresh stuff you buy in the supermarket because they are processed and frozen so quickly after they're picked. Frozen peas and mixed vegetables are particularly handy for adding to just about any dish – or microwaving in small portions to serve on the side.

 Defining idea... **'A clever cook can make good meat of a whetstone.'**
DESIDERIUS ERASMUS (1466–1536)
Dutch priest and scholar

Frozen berries

A handful of frozen, mixed summer berries is great blended with natural yogurt to make a smoothie. Alternatively, defrost a portion and use to top porridge, custard, ice cream or pancakes.

Q   **I often use ready-made pasta sauces – can they be a healthy option?**

How did it go?

A   I always keep stir-in pasta sauces in my cupboard. Not the huge jars of cheap, creamy, cheesy stuff – but the smaller, pesto-sized jars of organic tomato or vegetable-based sauce. These are invaluable for a quick supper – but be warned, a little goes a long way. I prefer to dilute their powerful, slightly acidic flavour by adding an equal quantity of half fat fromage frais and a sprinkle of parmesan when I stir them into cooked pasta.

For a more rounded meal, I usually add finely chopped vegetables to the boiling pasta a few minutes before it's finished cooking too – then possibly add some strips of chopped ham or roast chicken when I add the sauce, warming the whole lot up again on a low heat. Don't add salt to your cooking water if you're using something like this – the sauce and the parmesan will provide more than enough.

Q   **What about the sauces you find in tubs in the chiller cabinets in supermarkets?**

A   Some of those are great – and can be frozen, which makes them really handy. As with any food, read the labels to check exactly what's in it. Compare a couple of sauces and then choose the healthiest.

121

28
Hello, Mr Chips!

You don't have to take chips off the menu if you want to feed your family well – just choose carefully.

Most kids love chips — and the good news is, if you make the right choice, they're not as unhealthy as you might think.

This doesn't mean you should feed your child chips every day! However, a small portion of the right sort of chips – served alongside other healthy, non-fried foods such as grilled fish or chicken, a lean, grilled beef burger and of course, some vegetables or salad – is not only going to make you popular, but it won't do your kids any harm now and then, either.

Follow this guide to the best chip choices around. They are listed, starting with the healthiest then working down in descending order, to the most unhealthy choice for your family.

HOME-MADE, BAKED 'CHIPS'

These 'chips' have the lowest fat and highest fibre and vitamin content of all – especially if you use fresh potatoes and cook them immediately after preparing them. An average portion of baked 'chips' (ok, let's be honest – they're wedges) can

Here's an idea for you... **Ring the changes by using sweet potatoes. Whilst they don't make great conventional chips, they do taste delicious cut into wedges, parboiled for five minutes, dried, then coated in a little olive oil and baked for 15 minutes at 200°C/400°F/Gas 6.**

contain less fat than a jacket potato topped with a knob of butter.

… Preheat your oven to 230°C/450°F/Gas 8. Use large potatoes and scrub well. According to the British Potato Council, King Edwards make the best chips – with Maris Piper, the chip shops' favourite variety, running a close second.

Keeping the skin on (many of the potato's nutrients are stored just under the skin), slice the potatoes in half lengthways, then slice each half into 6–8 long wedges. Pat dry, then place the wedges in a bowl with just a splash of oil (you just want to give them the thinnest of coats). Use your hands to toss them until they are lightly coated in oil – then place on a baking sheet and bake for 30 minutes or so until golden, turning half way through the cooking time.

Top tip

To preserve the potato's valuable nutrients peel the potato just before cooking – don't leave them exposed to the air or standing in water any longer than you have to.

READY-MADE OVEN CHIPS

Chunky, straight-cut oven chips have the lowest calorie/fat content of all the ready-made chips (their nutritional profile is pretty similar to the home-made baked version, above) as they are just potato brushed with oil. Avoid crinkle cuts and thin cut fries however, as they have more surface area, and so absorb more fat.

MICROWAVE CHIPS

Although this kind of chipped spud is thin cut, if you stick to a small portion it can be a reasonable option. When it comes to their fat content, they fall somewhere between oven-baked and fried chips. Despite their junk-food appearance, they are made with just potato and vegetable oil – so not as bad as they look. Watch out for the new, big, fat microwave chips however, they contain extra additives to give them a crunchy coating – and they come in a bigger portion size.

FRIED, HOME MADE CHIPS

Cut your chips thickly and fry them straight away (drying them thoroughly first), ideally from room temperature, in small batches, and in very hot oil if you want them to absorb less fat and retain as many vitamins as possible.

On the other hand, if you want to fry the 'perfect' traditional 'chef's' chip, without worrying too much about leaching vitamins and a little more fat – follow this method recommended by the experts.

Peel and slice your potatoes, then soak them in cold water for 20 minutes or more to remove excess starch. Just before you're

Avoid adding salt to chips. To find out why, read IDEA 21, Pass the salt.

Try another idea…

"French fries. I love them. Some people are chocolate and sweets people. I love French fries. That and caviar."
CAMERON DIAZ

Defining idea…

125

ready to cook them, drain and pat dry thoroughly. Next, fry them in vegetable oil at 170°C/325°F for 4–6 minutes, lifting them out just before they start to colour. Turn the heat up to 190°C/375°F and then put them back in the oil for 2–3 minutes until golden. Drain on kitchen roll and serve.

BURGER BAR FRIES

On a par with frozen chips (see below), for their high calorie and fat content – the thin cut of these fries means they contain a paticularly high proportion of grease. Whilst most burger chains now use a healthier oil with less cholesterol-boosting trans fats, these chips do tend to be heavily salted, which is never a good thing.

CHIP SHOP CHIPS

With one of the highest fat contents, chip shop chips can also be fried in oil with a relatively high, unhealthy trans fat content and some are still fried in animal fats, which are high in saturates. These chips are also often low in vitamin C because of the time the cut potatoes spend hanging around before they get fried.

FROZEN CHIPS FOR FRYING

These are not as healthy as oven, microwave or home-made chips – even if you choose a thick cut variety. The reason is, frozen chips cool down the frying oil – so they don't seal quickly, which means they absorb more fat than chip shop and burger bar chips.

Q   What oil should I fry my chips in? Is olive oil OK?

How did it go?

A   *Olive oil is not suitable for frying chips. As a monounsaturated oil it has a low smoking point. Groundnut (peanut) is the oil of choice, as it has a very bland flavour (although it's not suitable for children with a nut allergy) – however, sunflower, corn or vegetable oil work well too.*

Q   Can I reuse the oil once I've cooked the chips?

A   *Yes. Allow the oil to cool, then filter it to remove any debris. Store in a bottle in a cool, dark place (not the fridge, as oil starts to solidify when it gets too cold). Do not reuse cooking oil too many times, however, as it will start to degrade and form unhealthy trans fatty acids. Throw it away once it starts to discolour.*

127

29
Chicken tonight

Quick and versatile to cook with – chicken is the must-have main ingredient for a host of delicious, healthy meals.

From home-made nuggets, to fajitas and chicken with rice — you really can't go wrong with any of these popular family dishes.

The first thing to know about chicken, however, is that it can vary enormously in taste and texture, depending on the quality of bird that you buy. Your average supermarket, factory-farmed chicken will tend to be on the dry, flavourless, fatty side, as birds are often raised with the help of growth promoting hormones and then killed relatively early – at just 42 days old. These type of birds are also usually farmed indoors, in cramped cages with the help of daily doses of drugs to stave off disease.

Free-range, organic chicken on the other hand tends to be more tasty, as birds have to be reared for at least 81 days before they are killed. Growth-promoting drugs are banned and the birds are usually allowed outdoors on a daily basis, with access to grass and freedom to roam.

Whilst organic, free-range chicken can, unfortunately, cost almost twice as much as the ordinary sort – personally, I think it's worth paying the extra.

Leftover roast chicken (or even ready-cooked roast chicken slices) can be used to make a number of quick dishes:

- **Chop and add, along with a handful of frozen peas, enough good quality chicken or mushroom soup to make a 'sauce' – heat through and serve over rice.**
- **To make a pasta sauce – chop roast chicken and mix with pesto, some fromage frais and roast vegetables.**
- **Finely chop roast chicken then mix into mashed potatoes with some mashed steamed broccoli. Form into 'cakes', roll in breadcrumbs and bake in a 200°C/400°F/Gas Mark 6 oven for 25 minutes.**

One of the best ways to serve chicken to children is to give it a bit of extra flavour by marinating it for at least an hour before cooking. Twelve or twenty-four hours in the marinade is even better (you can also freeze the chicken in these marinades – then take out portions to defrost and cook when you need them).

Coat two skinned drumsticks or one skinned chicken breast in one of the following marinades (chicken skin is high in saturated – unhealthy – fat, so best removed). Of course, you can expand the recommended amounts to coat more pieces of chicken if you wish. Cover with cling film and refrigerate until ready to cook.

Marinaded chicken is best grilled under a medium heat, on a rack over a baking tray – to catch the drips.

Try mixing together:

- A tablespoon of ketchup, a tablespoon of runny honey, a crushed garlic clove and teaspoon of olive oil.

- A tablespoon of runny honey, a table-spoon of soy sauce, an inch of fresh ginger, grated, (scrape pieces of ginger off the chicken before you cook it) and a tea-spoon of vegetable oil.
- 2 tablespoons of natural yogurt and 1 tablespoon of mango chutney.
- 1 tablespoon each of peanut butter and apple juice, a teaspoon of soy sauce and a teaspoon of muscovado sugar.

For more information on freezing food – turn to IDEA 51 *The big freeze.*

Try another idea…

Children will also enjoy assembling mild 'chicken fajitas' in their soft bread wraps. To serve two to four – depending on appetite – cut two skinless chicken breasts into strips, place in a bowl, then coat with a marinade of the juice of one lime, a table-spoon of vegetable oil, a teaspoon of dried oregano, a teaspoon of dried coriander and a crushed garlic clove. Cover the chicken and the marinade with cling film and refrigerate for at least an hour. Just before you are ready to cook the chicken, gently fry a large onion and a de-seeded red pepper – both finely sliced – in a little olive oil, until they are soft. Remove vegetables from the pan then fry the chicken (having shaken off any excess marinade) until cooked through. Return the vegetables to the pan and mix with the chicken. Serve with soft tortillas, and help-yourself bowls of half-fat creme fraiche, mashed avocado and tomato salsa.

'Is there chicken in chick peas?'
HELEN ADAMS, *Big Brother* 2001 contestant

Defining idea…

131

How did
it go?

Q   My children love chicken nuggets. I know most of the shop-bought and fast food nuggets are made with the minced up chicken bits no one wants to eat – but I'm finding it impossible to ban their favourite food. Any suggestions?

A   *I've yet to meet a child who doesn't like chicken nuggets. Of course, it's extremely tempting to keep a box of the frozen, shop-bought variety in the freezer. But as you say, you have no real way of knowing what's in them. So have a go at making your own – it really is as quick and easy as bunging a handful of frozen, mass-produced ones on a baking tray, and they taste just as good, if not better.*

To make one large, or two small servings of nuggets, pre-heat your oven to 200°C/400°F/Gas Mark 6. Lightly toast two slices of white bread, and then grind them into fine crumbs in a food processor along with a good pinch of garlic powder and a pinch of paprika. Cut a skinless, boneless chicken breast into cubes (I use kitchen scissors) and immerse the pieces in a bowl containing one egg beaten with 2 tablespoons of milk. Drain the chicken, then coat with the breadcrumbs. Place the breaded chicken pieces on an oiled baking sheet and bake for 12–15 minutes until cooked through.

Q   Will these nuggets freeze, so I don't have to make a fresh batch every time?

A   *Yes. I would freeze them individually on a tray for a couple of hours, then quickly pack the loose nuggets in an airtight bag or container and replace in the freezer. They should be OK for up to 3 months. Remember to defrost them thoroughly before cooking.*

30
Pasta

For a fantastic family meal or single portion home-cooked supper in less than 15 minutes – choose pasta.

Spinach, broccoli, fish — you'll be amazed at what your child will eat if it's turned into a sauce and poured over pasta.

Don't think that you need to make your own pasta or even buy it fresh. On the contrary. In Italy, good quality dried pasta is the order of the day for almost every dish – with the exception of filled pasta like ravioli and tortellini. So keep your store cupboard stocked with a variety of child-pleasing dried pasta shapes and you'll be able to knock up a multitude of popular dishes – for any number of kids – in no time.

Look for farfalle (pasta bows), conchiglie (shells) and rotelle (wagon wheels) and of course, spaghetti and macaroni. For smaller children think fusillini (tiny twists), farfalline (mini bows) and conchigliette (tiny shells), which are now widely available and take just 4–5 minutes to cook. Available from larger supermarkets and some healthfood stores, Pasta Pals Organic pasta shapes are really worth looking out for as they come in dinosaur, animal and alphabet letters.

Fun or unusual shaped pasta is a really worthwhile investment when it comes to getting your child interested in a meal. Whilst many supermarkets offer a wide selection of child-friendly shapes and baby pastas, they can sometimes be hard to find. If you're passing, always be sure to check the selections in Italian delis and upmarket food halls, and if you're on holiday in Europe, the local supermarket is always worth a quick look. If you find a shape you think your kids will love, stock up – buying at least one more bag than you think you'll need.

Soft, well-cooked pasta is also a great first food for babies of nine months or more – once you feel she is ready to graduate from purée and baby rice to something with a little more bite. Look for tiny soup pasta, often in the shape of stars (stelline), hoops (anellini) or letters of the alphabet – or specially made baby pasta. You can buy boxes of Italian baby pasta as well as every other shape and size of pasta online from www.nifeislife.com – a website that specialises in Italian food.

For babies, mix cooked pasta into loose vegetable purées or serve, well cooked and topped with a little butter and finely grated cheese. Some mums say their finger-food eating babies enjoy chewing on larger, more robust pieces of well-cooked pasta such as the odd pasta tube or twist as an alternative to breadsticks, rice cakes and carrot batons (however, never leave your young child alone when she is eating – whatever she is eating – in case she starts to choke).

Once you've chosen your pasta, you can top it in a number of simple ways. A small knob of butter, splash of olive oil and sprinkle of dried sage and parmesan is super-quick and delicious.

To make a great Bolognese sauce turn to IDEA 35, *Meaty issues*.

Try another idea…

Most kids seem to like pesto too – though I sometimes tone down its powerful flavour with an equal quantity of mascarpone, fromage frais or even cream cheese.

A simple tomato sauce (which you can make loads of and freeze in small portions) is an indispensable topping – as you can eat it with a sprinkle of parmesan or add all kinds of good things to it. To make a batch of sauce – finely chop and then sauté a medium onion and two cloves of garlic until soft. Add a tin of chopped tomatoes with herbs, a tin full of water and a tablespoon of tomato purée. Simmer for 20–30 minutes until all the tomato pieces have softened – then serve or cool and decant into pots for the freezer.

Tasty additions to tomato sauce include small 'meatballs' made by opening up a sausage or two and hand rolling the meat into balls (fry before adding them to the sauce); flaked tuna; small pieces of steamed mixed veg (purée and stir in if necessary); cream cheese and chopped roast chicken.

'Everything you see I owe to spaghetti.'

SOPHIA LOREN

Defining idea…

135

How did it go?

Q   It's sounds ridiculous, but I never seem to be able to cook pasta 'just right'. It always ends up stuck together in one gloopy mass. Someone told me I should add a tablespoon of oil to the water whilst it's cooking to stop it sticking. Is that right?

A   *Oil is unnecessary – and tends to stop the sauce clinging to the pasta once it's cooked. The key to well-cooked, non-stick pasta is to use a big pan and plenty of water so that there's a lot of room for the pasta to move freely and remain separate whilst it's cooking. By eye, I'd recommend at least four times as much water as pasta.*

Make sure the water is at a rolling boil before you add the pasta (it's best not to salt the water for children's meals). Keep the heat on full to return the water to a boil as quickly as possible once the pasta has been added. Stir the pasta just once, then turn it down to a vigorous simmer. Cook for the recommended time, then drain – but not too thoroughly. Keeping a little cooking water with the pasta will also help to stop it sticking. Add your sauce, heat through – and allow to sit for a minute so that the pasta is nice and soft.

Q   But shouldn't pasta be served *al dente* – slightly undercooked, with a firm bite to it?

A   *If you like it al dente – fine. However, I think you'll find your children will prefer their pasta soft and well-cooked. It's easier to eat.*

NB Gluten-containing foods such as pasta are not suitable for children under six months. If you have a family history of wheat allergy or coeliac disease, consult your GP before giving your child gluten-containing foods.

31
Rice is nice

Don't be put off by rice's 'difficult' reputation. Kids will love this versatile food.

A delicious, low fat carbohydrate food, packed with vitamins — cooking with rice really can be child's play.

PERFECT RICE

The ideal accompaniment to curry, chilli con carne, roast vegetables, stir fries, stewed chicken and even grilled fish.

- Basmati is the best rice to use for separate, fluffy grains.
- Always use a measuring jug, rather than the scales, to work out how much rice and liquid you need. It's one part rice to two parts liquid. For a child, that's roughly 55ml/2fl oz of rice per person to 110ml/4fl oz liquid.
- The best pan to use to cook rice in is a non-stick, wide-bottomed one with a lid (a frying pan with a lid is ideal).
- Add a little oil to the pan first, and lightly 'fry' the grains for a few seconds so they are coated in oil, not browned, before adding the right amount of boiling water or hot stock. You could soften some finely chopped onions, leeks, garlic, or vegetables in the oil before adding the rice for extra flavour. Try tossing in a little desiccated coconut, chopped apricots or raisins before the liquid for a sweeter flavour.

Here's an idea for you... **Brown rice is packed with vitamins and fibre and can be used in place of Basmati – it just takes much longer to cook (see pack for timings). It can even be use for rice pudding – just boil it in plain water for 30 minutes before adding it to the milk and sugar and baking.**

- Once the boiling liquid has been added, stir once, cover and leave to simmer on the very lowest heat. Do not lift the lid or stir again until the recommended cooking time has elapsed.
- Tilt the pan to see if all the liquid has been absorbed. If it hasn't, give the rice a couple more minutes.
- Remove the lid and cover with a clean tea towel to absorb excess steam. Just before serving, fluff the grains with a fork.

RISOTTO

Once you've got this simple, basic recipe right, you can add just about anything you like to it to make really delicious, economical meals from very few ingredients.

To make a basic risotto for four, first, gently sweat a large red onion, a couple of celery sticks and a carrot – all finely chopped – in a tablespoon of olive oil in a large, non-stick saucepan. Once cooked, but not browned, add two finely chopped cloves of garlic and fry for another minute or so. (While the vegetables are cooking make around 1½ litres (3 pints) stock – choose the flavour to fit the other ingredients you're going to add – and keep it hot). Now turn up the heat a little and add 400g/14oz risotto rice (look for arborio, carnaroli or vialone nano) to the vegetables, and fry the rice, stirring all the time until it looks translucent. Keeping the rice on a medium to low-ish heat, start adding the stock a ladleful at a time, stirring the rice until each ladle of stock has been absorbed before adding the next. Keep doing this for 20–25 minutes. You may have some stock left over – but don't worry. Let the rice guide you – it will only absorb as much liquid as it wants to, not as much as you tell it to. Add any extra ingredients half way through the cooking time – try a handful of small broccoli florets; chopped baby spinach; sliced asparagus; finely snipped, lean, cooked bacon; chopped roast chicken; small prawns; even chopped chorizo. Once the rice is cooked

Rice milk can be a useful alternative for some kids with dairy allergies – see IDEA 5, *I think I'm going to be sick!*

Try another idea…

– it should be creamy and just slightly sloppy – stir in a tablespoon each of half fat fromage frais and grated parmesan. Leave to sit for five minutes before stirring again and serving.

RICE PUDDING

Eat it for dessert or store it in the fridge in individual portions (having sneakily eaten the skin first yourself) for handy snacks, lunchbox desserts, bedtime suppers or served with chopped fruit for an instant breakfast. So simple, your child can measure the ingredients and 'make' it himself (with you doing the oven bit, obviously). To serve 4–6, put 75g/3oz pudding rice, a heaped tablespoon sugar, 150ml/¼ pint evaporated milk and 450ml/¾ pint whole milk and a knob of butter in a medium ovenproof dish – stir, then top with grated nutmeg. Place on the middle shelf 150°C/300°F/Gas 2, untouched, for 2–3 hours.

EGG FRIED RICE

A great way to use up cold, leftover rice. Using enough rice to serve two, beat together a large egg with a teaspoon of sesame oil. Heat a wok or large saucepan until very hot then add a scant tablespoon of groundnut (peanut) or sunflower oil. Once the oil is almost smok-

'Rice is the best, the most nutritive and unquestionably the most widespread staple in the world.'

GEORGES AUGUSTE ESCOFFIER, legendary chef (1846–1935)

Defining idea…

ing, throw in the rice (and any other suitable leftovers – finely chopped) and stir fry for three minutes until thoroughly heated. Pour in the egg mixture and stir fry for three more minutes. Stir in a dash of dark or reduced salt soy sauce, black pepper and a finely chopped spring onion and serve.

How did it go?

Q **Why do you recommend Basmati rice? Isn't it quicker to use easy cook or boil-in-the-bag?**

A *Basmati is one of the best quality types of rice you can buy. You simply won't get the same results or taste with the processed versions. I reckon the difference is worth the extra 2–5 minutes cooking time.*

Q **No matter how careful I am, I always end up cooking too much rice. I heard you shouldn't really keep it as it can harbour dangerous bacteria. Is that right?**

A *That's right – you must be careful when storing cooked rice. It will keep well in a sealed container in the fridge until the next day – but you must cool it quickly (rinse it with cold water) before storing it immediately in the fridge. If you're not then using it for a cold rice salad, make sure you reheat it really thoroughly so it's piping hot all the way through.*

32

Spuds they'll like

**Can't think of a thing to cook – indeed, can't be
bothered to cook? Before you reach for that microwave
meal, think spuds.**

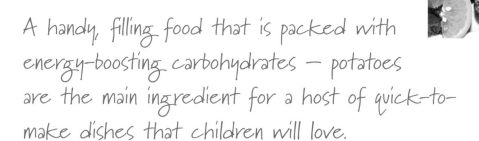

A handy, filling food that is packed with
energy-boosting carbohydrates — potatoes
are the main ingredient for a host of quick-to-
make dishes that children will love.

Potatoes are a starchy carbohydrate food – containing some protein, no fat, lots of
fibre and a wide range of vitamins including vitamin C.

Potato skin is a good source of fibre, and the flesh just under the skin is where most
of the vitamin C is stored – so do try to use scrubbed, unpeeled potatoes wherever
possible (although this may not be possible for younger children).

A portion of new potatoes contains more vitamin C than two fresh apples. They
taste great boiled, with their skins on – even when cold. For healthy 'roast potatoes'
– boil the potatoes, drain, then toss in a little olive oil, crushed garlic and sprinkle of

Here's an
idea for
you...

According to the experts at the British Potato Council, you will keep potatoes in top condition for longer if you remove them from their plastic bag as soon as you get home. Store them in a cloth or natural fibre bag – somewhere cool, dark and dry. Do not keep them in the fridge (it can cause them to degrade more quickly) and avoid storing them near other, strongly flavoured foods, such as onions.

dried rosemary and bake for 20–30 minutes. You could even try threading boiled new potatoes onto wooden skewers with small cooked chipolatas and pieces of sweet red pepper for fun-to-eat kebabs.

Most kids love mashed potato and so should you, as mash makes a brilliant base for a multitude of delicious, filling meals for young children.

The easiest way to make 'mash' – particularly if you are cooking for just one or two small children – is to zap a large baking potato in a microwave for 10–12 minutes. Peel and then mash the flesh with a small knob of butter before adding the 'topping' of your choice. Baked beans and a little grated cheese such as emmental or mild cheddar always go down well. A small can of tuna (canned in spring water) mixed with a little mayonnaise and sweetcorn; fresh tomato and mascarpone pasta sauce (from the chiller cabinet in your supermarket); or add puréed vegetables and a dash of milk to make a gloopy, lump-free weaning food.

For older children, who may like to eat a proper baked potato with crispy skin, bake your potatoes for 1 ½–2 hours in a hot oven, having coated the skins with a little olive oil and dash of sea salt first. Once cooked, let your child fill her own baked spud. Split, and mash in a little butter, then add one of the above fillings or try pesto and chopped roast chicken, a little fried (but not browned) minced garlic and cheese, chopped ham and cheese, or flavoured cream cheese.

To find – and cook – the perfect chip read IDEA 28, *All about chips*.

Try another idea...

Mashed potato is also the main ingredient in fishcakes – which are incredibly easy to make. Making these family favourites yourself means you know exactly what your child is eating – and you can tailor their size to her appetite. Older children will also enjoy helping to make these as there's lots of mashing and shaping to do.

FISH CAKES

Peel and boil potatoes until they're tender – you'll need four medium sized potatoes to 500g/1lb fish – then mash with a raw egg and the flaked fish of your choice. Poach cod or haddock for a few minutes in boiling milk then drain before using – or use drained, canned salmon or tuna. Add a little pepper, a dash of lemon juice and a good sprinkling of parsley (even some chopped, steamed veggies) – then shape the mixture into cakes. Roll the cakes in flour – or dip in egg and then breadcrumbs. Fry in a little hot vegetable oil over a medium heat until browned and cooked through (approximately three minutes each side), serve with ketchup or tartare sauce and veggies.

'Only two things in this world are too serious to be jested on, potatoes and matrimony.'
Irish saying

Defining idea...

143

How did it go?

Q **My children love mash – but whenever I try and make it, I end up with an undercooked, lumpy mess or a saucepan full of useless potato slush. What am I doing wrong?**

A *Different varieties of potato have different textures – which means some lend themselves better to certain cooking methods than others. For great mash, roasts and chips seek out King Edwards or Desiree. Also good for mash and boiling are Estima and Maris Piper. Charlotte, Maris Peer and Nicola varieties are excellent for salads. For superb baked potatoes try Estima again or creamy Marfona.*

Q **Actually I usually use King Edwards, which I know are pretty versatile. I just seem to be unable to boil them until they're just right.**

A *Then the trick is to be sure you cut the potatoes to the right size and steam rather than boil them.*
   Cut your potatoes too small and they will absorb large quantities of water and go slushy – too large, and it'll take ages for them to cook through. Using King Edwards or Desiree, peel sparingly then quarter the larger potatoes and halve smaller ones.
   To cook, place the potato pieces in a steamer over a pan of boiling water, put on a lid and steam for 20–25 minutes. Check if they're ready by piercing the largest potato piece with a knife or skewer through its thickest part. When it feels tender, they're ready to be mashed with a little butter and milk.

33

Vegging out

So your child has turned veggie? He won't end up malnourished, and you won't have to soak enormous pans of chickpeas overnight if you follow this advice.

With a bit of research and planning, a vegetarian diet can be a healthy, delicious and hassle-free choice.

Yes, a vegetarian diet can be a healthy, but only as long as a balanced diet is followed (i.e. plenty of carbohydrates, fruit and vegetables, reasonable amounts of protein and dairy and very small amounts of sugary and fatty foods).

If your child does not have a vegetarian family background, his diet will need some gentle supervision at first. If meat is simply left out of main meals and not replaced with a suitable vegetarian alternative, nutritional shortfalls can occur. In particular:

■ *Protein*: meat and fish are the main sources of protein in a regular, omnivorous diet. Beans, nuts, seeds, eggs, soya, cheese and rice are all foods that will add useful protein to a child's vegetarian diet. The meat in many family favourites such as bolognese, cottage pie, chilli and lasagne can easily be replaced with beans, soya mince or Quorn mince. Look out for veggie alternatives to sausages and burgers in your supermarket too.

- *Iron*: teenage girls are particularly at risk of iron deficiency, due to blood losses at menstruation. Red meat, liver and oily fish are all rich in iron, but vegetarians can turn to egg yolks, beans, lentils, fortified breakfast cereals, green vegetables and bread for good iron sources. Vitamin C enhances the absorption of iron, so it makes sense to serve fresh fruit juice or fresh fruit with meals.

- *Calcium*: all children need plenty of bone-building calcium in their diet. Teen-agers need particularly high levels – around 800–1000g during rapid growth periods, when 45% of the strength of their adult skeleton is laid down. Good vegetarian sources of calcium include cows' milk, fortified soya milk, cheese, yoghurt and all dairy products, white bread, green vegetables, tofu, dried fruit, almonds and wholemeal bread.

- *Zinc*: zinc is important for growth and cell division. as well as sexual maturation, especially in males. Poor dietary intakes of zinc can lower the body's immune response and leads to an increase in common infections. Insufficient zinc at a time of rapid growth can also cause growth problems. Vegetarian children should be encouraged to eat plenty of cheese, pumpkin seeds, pulses, nuts and tofu.

- *Vitamin B12*: important in the formation of blood cells and nerves, this vitamin is found mostly in animal foods, but vegetarian sources are supplied by dairy products, fortified breakfast cereals and eggs.

Here's an idea for you...

For more information on feeding vegetarian children (and advice for vegetarian children themselves), The Vegetarian Society produce helpful leaflets and have a useful website and email enquiry service (helpline: 0161 925 2000 or www.vegsoc.org).

Just as living on nothing but beef burgers is a bad idea – living on just cheese and salad is a bad idea too. Variety is the key to any healthy diet – vegetarian included. So as long as your child eats plenty of different foods you can be sure he will be getting all the nutrients he needs.

EATING WELL

For advice on feeding younger vegetarian children turn back to IDEA 4, *Veggie mites*.

Try another idea...

If you think about it, a fair number of the meals you already make are probably vegetarian – and many of your family favourites will probably adapt well. If you're still not sure what to give your child to eat, begin by asking him what he'd like. Buy a big veggie cookbook with plenty of photographs for inspiration and go shopping together to get a good idea of the vegetarian foods on offer. Involve other family members too by having vegetarian nights at home when they can choose their favourite dishes.

QUICK FIXES

Whilst a good vegetarian recipe book will prove invaluable now – if you're looking for a quick lunch, supper or snack, you can't go wrong with one of these suggestions:

- Jacket potatoes cooked in the microwave – serve with baked beans and cheese/hummus/tinned ratatouille/veggie chilli.
- Scrambled eggs on toast with tomatoes on the side.
- Cheese on toast with a side salad.
- Soup – try mushroom/vegetable/tomato and mascarpone/asparagus/broccoli and cheese – with a hunk of fresh bread.
- Sandwiches filled with egg/vegetarian pate/guacamole/hummus.
- Pasta with pesto.
- Stir fried vegetables with noodles – toss in a handful of peanuts or cashews.
- Omelette with wild mushrooms/garlic and spinach/chopped peppers.

'Nothing will benefit human health and increase chances for survival of life on Earth as much as the evolution to a vegetarian diet.'
ALBERT EINSTEIN

Defining idea...

147

- Veggie burger in a wholegrain roll with salad and coleslaw.
- Veggie sausage in a hot dog roll.
- Poached egg and beans.

How did it go?

Q My daughter won't eat jelly sweets because she says they contain gelatine. Are there any other animal ingredients I need to be aware of in foods?

A Gelatine is made from animal skin, tendons and bones and is often found in jelly, puddings and sweets. Another ingredient to avoid is 'animal fat'. Not to be confused with vegetable fat or butter, animal fat is carcass fat and can be found in cakes, biscuits and some puddings. Some cheese contains rennet, obtained from calves' stomachs – so look for cheese labelled as suitable for vegetarians to be absolutely sure. Some E numbers, such as E120, can have an animal origin too.

Q Is there any way I can get around having to read food labels in fine detail?

A Look out for the Vegetarian Society's seedling logo. This stamp of approval means foods have met four strict criteria: suitable for vegetarians, GM free, cruelty-free – and if eggs have been used, they must be free-range. If there's a product you are unsure of you can call the manufacturers customer care line listed on the packet. They should be able to tell you if their product is suitable for vegetarians.

34

Fishing for compliments

From hake to sole, to sardines and monkfish – there are shoals of tasty fish varieties out there just waiting to be turned into healthy, child-friendly meals.

So, don't limit your repertoire to ready-made fish cakes and fish fingers — push the boat out!

Fish is an excellent source of protein, B vitamins, the antioxidant selenium and minerals. Low in saturated fat – oily fish, such as salmon, herrings, mackerel and tuna also has the bonus of being a good source of healthy omega-3 fatty acids, which may help to reduce the risk of heart disease.

Fish with edible bones, such as sardines, pilchards and tinned salmon, also contain calcium, phosphorus and fluoride. Calcium is needed for healthy bones, phosphorus is essential for many body functions and fluoride helps to keep teeth strong.

So when can you start to put fish on your child's menu? Babies under six months shouldn't be given fish at all. However, from 6–9 months you can offer white fish such as cod, haddock and coley – but no oily fish. From 9–12 months you can start to introduce oily fish such as fresh tuna, salmon, mackerel and sardines.

Here's an idea for you... **Take your child to the fish counter of a large supermarket or a local fishmongers at a quiet time of day and ask the fishmonger to show her all the different fish before she picks one for her tea (most fishmongers will fillet your choice for you if you're squeamish).**

For small children, flake all fish really carefully once it's cooked to make sure there are absolutely no bones in it. Buy boned fish and warn older children to look out for stray bones whilst they're eating.

Although shellfish are low in fat and high in protein, vitamins and minerals, they are one of the foods most likely to provoke an allergic reaction – and so are best left off the menu until your child is 12 months old.

The UK Food Standards Agency advise that children under the age of 16 should not eat marlin, swordfish or shark as they may contain higher- than-recommended levels of mercury. Pregnant women and women wishing to get pregnant should also avoid eating these three fish for the same reason.

So let's get cooking.

SALMON IN A BAG (SERVES 4)

Children will love putting together their own supper 'bag' (just remember to score everyone's initials into the foil so you know whose is whose).

Preheat the oven to 190°C/375°F/Gas 5. Cut 4 large pieces of foil, big enough to loosely wrap four salmon fillets. Place a salmon fillet (or fish of your choice) in the centre of each piece of foil on a baking tray, then gently bring up the sides of the foil to create a loose bowl effect. Squeeze over a little lemon juice, toss in some finely sliced salad onions and whatever else you fancy – perhaps some chopped sun dried tomatoes, a sprinkling of dill and some capers a little finely sliced pancetta and tarragon. Now fold over the foil to create a tight seal, leaving a bit of air space inside the parcel. Place in the oven and bake for 15–20 minutes – until cooked through.

CHEAT'S FISH PIE (SERVES 1)

This is an easy-to-put-together comfort food, and you can expand the quantities according to the number of people you wish to feed.

Make up a portion of mashed potato. Next, boil a portion of boneless white fish, such as cod, haddock or hoki, in a little milk with a handful of frozen peas and tiny carrot cubes for 3–5 minutes, until the fish is cooked through. Drain and flake the fish then place it with the vegetables in a small ovenproof dish with a tablespoon of the milk. Top with mashed potato and grated cheddar and grill until bubbly.

EASY FISH RICE (SERVES 4–6)

A simple lunch or supper that will suit the whole family

Heat a little oil in a large frying pan and gently fry a chopped red onion until soft. Add 110g/4oz chopped bacon to the pan and fry until cooked. Meanwhile poach 1lb/450g skinned and cubed coley or haddock in a little water until cooked. Add 175g/6oz frozen mixed vegetables, 175g/6oz pre-cooked rice, 50g/2oz chopped dried apricots, ½ tsp turmeric and cook for 5 minutes, stirring occasionally. Finally gently stir in the drained, cooked fish and serve.

For a simple fish cake recipe look at IDEA 32, *Spuds they'll like.*

Try another idea...

'In the hands of an able cook, fish can become an inexhaustible source of perpetual delight.'
JEAN-ANTHELME BRILLAT-SAVARIN, French food writer (1755–1826)

Defining idea...

How did it go?

Q   How many portions of fish should my child be eating a week?

A   The current recommendation is at least two portions of fish a week – one of which should be an oily fish. If your child suddenly develops a craving for mackerel or salmon however, it's worth noting that there are safety limits on the amount of oily fish he should eat. Boys, men, and women who aren't going to become pregnant in the future can eat up to four portions of oily fish a week. Girls, women who may want to have children in the future and breast-feeding mums should eat no more than two portions of oily fish a week.

Q   Why is there a recommended limit on oily fish?

A   Some oily fish can contain harmful chemicals, such as dioxins and PCBs. Dioxins are a by-product of certain industrial processes and household fires. PCBs (polychlorinated biphenyls) are pollutants used mainly in the production of electrical equipment. They are no longer permitted in the UK, but may still be present in the environment, including fish. Dioxins and PCBs do not have an immediate effect on health, but there is concern that higher than recommended levels in the diet over a long period of time may increase the risk of cancer.

Q   That sounds really scary!

A   Don't worry. Levels of PCBs and dioxins have started to fall recently, and supermarkets conduct stringent tests to ensure that the oily fish they sell fall within or below the minimum levels that are acceptable.

35

Meaty issues

Red meat has had a bad press over the last few years – but don't rule it out of your child's diet. It's a great source of important nutrients.

The best dietary source of easily absorbable iron and an excellent source of protein, B vitamins and other minerals, red meat can also be much lower in saturated fat than you might think.

Iron deficiency anaemia is quite common in some groups of young children such as those who are not receiving a good supply of iron from solid foods (other good sources of iron include fortified whole grain cereals and breads, lentils, beans and dried apricots) and those who are given cows' milk as a main drink too early (before 12 months). Iron deficiency can lead to frequent infections, poor weight gain and delay in development.

Suitable for children from 6 months old – there's no need to limit your child's red meat intake to sausages, however. Most children will eat small, finely chopped por-

Bacon can be popular with children – but choose carefully. Pick low fat cuts rather than streaky or middle and opt for the unsmoked version (smoked foods are thought by have possible carcinogenic effects, so are best avoided). Again, it's always a good idea to buy organic if possible. Look for reduced salt bacon too, as bacon does tend to be high in sodium.

tions of grilled lamb, pork and beef, casseroles, stir fries, shepherd's pie – and so on.

When buying meat, always look for lean, organic cuts. Trim away excess fat and remove further unwanted fat during cooking: grill chops and steaks and always skim fat from the top of stews, casseroles and meat sauces.

Home-made burgers are a simple way to get your child to eat red meat – and avoid the additives and fillers found in many shop-bought ones. You can also make your burgers exactly the right size for your child's appetite – so they're less wasteful too. Buy lean organic minced beef, pork or lamb and add the herbs, spices and even finely chopped, blanched vegetables of your choice before pressing the meat into a burger shape. A chopped onion and crushed garlic clove, both fried until soft, are essential flavouring for every type of burger mix – then try some additional basil and sundried tomato puree (ketchup will do) to beef, or a little apple sauce, mint and parsley with pork. A sprinkle of thyme and even some finely chopped feta cheese works well in lamb burgers.

If you find your burger mix too crumbly, add fresh bread crumbs and an egg to bind (approximately 2 tablespoons of bread crumbs and one egg for every 450g/1lb meat.

Shape your burgers to the size you prefer (allow your child to help with this – as long as he washes his hands thoroughly after touching the raw meat), then grill until cooked through. Serve in a bun with slices of tomato and cucumber or serve plain with cooked vegetables or reduced sugar, reduced salt baked beans on the side. Freeze uncooked burgers individually, then pack in an airtight bag, separated with leaves of greaseproof paper. Eat within a month.

Bolognese sauce is another sure-fire crowd pleaser which can be used on pasta or baked potatoes – and is really economical to make. I usually make a big batch for a family supper and then freeze the leftover sauce in small child-sized portions for later use. To serve 6–8 – with plenty left over – simply fry until soft a finely chopped onion, 2 crushed garlic cloves and 4 rashers of finely snipped bacon. Add 450g/1lb lean mince beef and fry on a medium heat until lightly browned – breaking up any lumps with a spoon as you go. Now stir in 2 large bottles of passata (sieved tomatoes), then fill one of the bottles with water and add that too. Add 2 teaspoons of dried oregano and a sprinkle of mixed herbs (add more herbs as the sauce cooks if you think it needs it) and a tablespoon each of tomato purée and Worcester sauce. Bring to a simmer, then place your pan on the smallest cooker ring and turn the heat down as low as it will go. For a tender, delicious sauce, allow the Bolognese to cook in this way, stirring occasionally and skimming off excess fat, for 2 hours. The sauce will be ready to eat after 30 minutes – but tastes much better if allowed to cook for much longer.

For meat of the non-red kind, read IDEA 29, *I feel like chicken tonight.*

Try another idea…

'Vegetables are interesting but lack a sense of purpose when unaccompanied by a good cut of meat.'
 FRAN LEBOWITZ, American humorist

Defining idea…

How did it go?

**Q   Can children eat liver? I loved liver as a child, but I read some-
where recently that it is very high in vitamin A – which can be
toxic in large quantities. I was advised not to eat liver during
pregnancy for this reason – so I wondered if it was safe for kids?**

A   *Liver is an excellent source of iron and can be given to children from 9
months onwards. Many children like it because it's soft to chew and easy to
eat. Because of its high vitamin A content, however, it's best not to offer
liver more than once every two weeks.*

**Q   Do you know what? I wouldn't have the foggiest idea how to
cook the stuff now. What are you supposed to do with it?**

A   *You can grill it, then chop it up finely, or dip thin slices in flour with a
sprinkle of sage added, then fry in butter until just cooked. It's nice with
sautéed onions or mushrooms and served with mash.*

**Q   I'm not convinced my daughter will eat it like that ... are there
any other ways to give it to her?**

A   *Well, you can always add some chopped liver to a vegetable or meat cas-
serole, stir fry or pasta sauce. Alternatively try a thin spread of liver pate in
sandwiches.*

36
Anything with a pulse

There are loads of different varieties of peas, beans and lentils, which can all be used in hundreds of interesting ways.

Don't dismiss pulses as boring old vegetarian fodder, because you'll be missing out on something really special.

A good source of protein, iron and fibre, beans and lentils work particularly well in soups and stews and can be a vital source of important nutrients for vegetarian children.

Dried pulses store well for long periods if kept in a dry, airtight container away from the light, but it's best to eat them sooner rather than later as they toughen with age and take longer to cook. With the exception of lentils, green and yellow split peas, blackeye and mung beans, most dried pulses need a long soak before they can be cooked (see pack for directions). Always discard the soaking water, then rinse and cook dried pulses in fresh water without any salt. Salt toughens the skins and makes for longer cooking.

Canned pulses, it has to be said, are much, much more convenient (look for no or low salt varieties). They're pre-soaked and cooked, so all you have to do is rinse and drain before use. Go on, try these recipes – beanz meanz happy kidz!

Red and yellow lentils cook down well and can be puréed with vegetables to make a more substantial baby food once weaning has been established for some time.

Kids will love growing their own beansprouts. Get hold of some mung beans – rinse, then soak in clean water for 12 hours. Rinse again, and pour the beans into a clean glass container. Cover the container with cling film to stop the beans drying out – and place on a cool, bright window ledge. Rinse the beans and replace in the container every morning and every evening (this is important to avoid mould formation). Within 4–5 days your beans should have started to germinate. Your crop is ready to eat when most of your sprouts have developed two small leaves. Beansprouts can be eaten raw as a snack, in sandwiches or in stir fries.

BEAN THERE, DONE THAT

Beanie burgers (makes 8)

This recipe is really easy for older children to make – with a little supervision of course.

Rinse and drain a can of black-eyed, haricot, kidney or flageolet beans, then mash them with a fork in a large bowl. Add a finely chopped small onion and red pepper, a cup of fresh breadcrumbs, 1 tsp dried mixed herbs, a squirt of tomato sauce and a beaten egg and mix well. Leave the mixture to sit for 5 minutes, then wet your hands to form the mix into burgers. Coat each one with a little flour – and brush with oil before putting under a grill for 4–5 minutes each side.

Chilli con carne (serves 6–8)

This tastes even better if it has been cooled, refrigerated and re-heated the next day – skip the cayenne and paprika if you're cooking for very young children

In a large pan, gently fry two finely chopped onions and three crushed garlic cloves in a little olive oil. Once the onion has softened stir in 2 tsps cumin, a tablespoon dried oregano and three bay leaves. Cook for a minute before adding 900g/2lb good quality minced beef. Brown meat in the pan – breaking up any lumps as you do so. Now add a tbsp paprika and a tsp cayenne pepper. Stir in 4 tablespoons of tomato puree, then tip in 3 ×

Use chick peas to make a quick hummus. Go to IDEA 39, Little dippers, for the recipe.

Try another idea...

400ml cans chopped tomatoes and 2 × 400ml cans of kidney beans and 300ml red wine. The wine is just for flavouring – the alcohol will boil off as the meat cooks. Now put a lid on and cook on a very low heat for 2 hours – checking and stirring it every 20–30 minutes. Serve piled in crisp tacos with salad, poured over baked potatoes or on rice, sprinkled with cheese.

Pasta e fagioli (pasta and beans) – (serves 4–6)

A traditional Italian soup-cum-pasta dish – this makes a great, soothing supper.

Heat 2 tbsp olive oil in a saucepan and sweat two finely chopped garlic cloves. Add a diced carrot, two peeled and diced potatoes a diced celery stick and a large tomato, deseeded and diced. Pour in 1.2L/2 pints chicken or vegetable stock and simmer for 5 minutes. Add a medium tin of drained borlotti beans to the stock, then mash another medium tin of drained borlotti beans to a pulp with the back of a fork (your child will enjoy doing that bit) and add to the stock with a little basil and 200g/7oz small pasta shapes (think mini fusilli and pennette). Cook on a low heat for 10 minutes, stirring from time to time. Remove any scum, add a splash of olive oil and serve.

'Lentils are friendly – the Miss Congeniality of the bean world.'
LAURIE COLWIN, food wrier and novelist (1944–1992)

Defining idea...

159

How did
it go?

Q **Are baked beans a good choice for children? Mine would eat them every day if they could.**

A   *Yes they are a good choice. Beans in tomato sauce are a low fat source of protein and contain good levels of iron, magnesium, fibre and the powerful antioxidant lycopene. On the down side, the regular version tends to be high in salt and sugar, so go for the reduced sugar and salt type every time, it's a worthwhile swap, health-wise. Please remember, a balanced diet means plenty of variety, so don't rely too heavily on family favourites like baked beans – ring the changes as often as possible.*

Q **Do pulses count towards the recommended five portions of fruit and veg a day?**

A   *Yes. Beans and pulses can count towards the five portions of fruit and veg we should aim to eat each day, but they can only make up a maximum of one portion a day, no matter how many times you have different beans and lentils during any particular day.*

37

Cheese please

A good source of calcium and popular with most children, cheese is a handy kitchen standby for creating tasty meals – fast.

So, why not tempt your kids away from those processed, stringy cheese sticks with a little imagination?

From six months of age you can start to introduce a little cheese into your child's diet, either blended into other foods or served in wafer thin slices or tiny cubes. As your child gets older, adding cheese to a dish is almost guaranteed to get him eating absolutely anything – even veggies.

Mould-ripened soft cheeses, such as Brie and Camembert and blue cheeses like Stilton and Gorgonzola, are not suitable until your child is at least 12 months old, however, as there is a risk that they can cause food poisoning in very young children.

Most types of cheese provide an excellent source of calcium – the mineral vital for bone strength and health. Cheese is also a relatively good source of protein, as well as some B vitamins and vitamin A.

Eating cheese after a meal has also been shown to help prevent tooth decay – and according to new research, a little cheese before bedtime does not give you nightmares. Its amino acid content can actually help reduce stress and improve sleep.

Here's an idea for you...

Give cheese on toast a sweet boost by adding apple or pear. Toast a slice of wholemeal bread, spread with a little butter then top with thin slices of sweet, dessert apple or pear. Sprinkle with a little grated cheese and a pinch of dried sage then grill until melted. Allow to cool for a minute or so before serving.

Aside from these benefits, however, cheese does tend to be high in saturated fat and salt – so is always best offered in moderation.

BASIC CHEESE SAUCE

Easy to make and super-versatile, this simple cheese sauce can be used to make any number of popular family dishes – from macaroni cheese to a quick lasagne (see below)

Place a 570ml/1 pint of whole milk, 40g/1½ oz plain flour and 40g/1½ oz butter in a non-stick saucepan and, using a balloon whisk, whisk the mixture as you bring it to a gentle simmer. Keep whisking until the sauce thickens, then stir with a wooden spoon as you allow the sauce to gently simmer for a further 5 minutes. Turn the heat off and immediately stir in a handful of mild Cheddar or half Cheddar/half Parmesan with a little ground black pepper and a heaped teaspoon of English mustard. Once the cheese has melted, the sauce can be used to make …

- Cauliflower cheese (serves 4–6). Break a large cauliflower into florets then boil for 3–4 minutes until just cooked, drain and pour over the hot cheese sauce (above). Sprinkle with bread crumbs and a little grated cheese and stick it under a hot grill to brown. (This recipe works equally well with a selection of vegetables – say, broccoli florets, carrot, peas and cauliflower if you prefer.)
- Macaroni cheese (serves 4–6). Stir the hot cheese sauce into 200g/7oz macaroni, (penne, rigatoni or pasta shells will also work well) that has been boiled and drained. Pour the mixture into a shallow baking dish and top with thin slices of tomato. Sprinkle with grated cheese and grill until browned.

- Quick lasagne (serves 4–6). Place a layer of ready-made tomato pasta sauce, a layer of cheese sauce, thin slices of ham, then a layer of lasagne sheets in a shallow baking dish – repeat layers, finishing with a layer of lasagne topped with tomato sauce then cheese sauce. Sprinkle with grated cheese and bake in the oven at 190°C/375°F/ Gas 5 for 40 minutes or so until cooked through and browned on the top.

Most cheeses have quite a high salt content – for information on controlling your child's salt intake read IDEA 21, *Pass the salt*.

Try another idea...

SPEEDY CHEESE AND BROCCOLI GNOCCHI

Drop a portion of gnocchi (Italian potato dumplings – widely available from super-market chilled sections) and a portion of broccoli florets (cut really small) into a pan of boiling water. Cook for 3–4 minutes (gnocchi are ready when they rise to the surface), drain and toss with a little butter and Parmesan – or the cheese of your choice.

Also good with hot gnocchi is butter, parmesan and a sprinkle of dried sage *or* pesto and a dab of mascarpone or fromage frais.

FAST 'PIZZA'

Home-made pizza makes a nutritious, filling snack, lunch or supper and kids love making their own. Cheat for speed and use toasted crumpets, English muffins, pitta breads, or french bread split lengthways for the base. Spread the toasted base with tomato purée or passata and then get creative with the toppings. Use roast chicken, chopped

'What happens to the holes when the cheese is gone?'
BERTOLT BRECHT, German dramatist (1898–1956)

Defining idea...

ham, tuna, mushrooms, sweet corn, sun dried tomatoes, olives – whatever they fancy – then sprinkle over thinly sliced mozzarella or grated cheese and a pinch or two of dried oregano. Grill until bubbling.

How did it go?

Q   My children love 'plastic' cheese – in particular those rubbery, stringy snacks and cheese spread. They are labelled as good sources of calcium, so are they a good idea – or should I try and steer them towards something else?

A   *Many cheese products that are aimed specifically at children, such as triangles, cheese spread, slices and strings, are best avoided as they tend to be highly processed and packed with saturated fat and salt.*

Q   Any suggestions for alternatives then? I would prefer them to eat 'real' cheese anyway.

A   *A good 'real' alternative to stringy cheese would be mozzarella (the soft balls of cheese that come packaged in liquid – rather than the pressed type you slice from a block). Mozzarella has a similar fun-to-eat texture. In place of cheese spread, triangles or cheese dips try Quark, half fat mascarpone or flavoured cottage cheese. Processed cheese slices can be replaced with ready cut slices of Cheddar, Leerdammer, Emmental or Edam.*

38
Egg them on

Probably one of the most versatile of kitchen ingredients, eggs are a good source of protein and a brilliant stand-by for a quick, healthy breakfast, lunch or supper.

However there are some rules that need to be followed, particularly when offering eggs to very young children.

Because of a very slight risk of salmonella food poisoning, it is recommended that children should not be given eggs until they are at least 6 months old. From 6–9 months you can give hard-cooked egg yolk, but experts advise avoiding egg white altogether at this age. From 9–12 months, you can give well-cooked egg white and well-cooked yolk. Avoid dishes containing raw egg such as mayonnaise and fresh chocolate mousse.

The Food Standards Agency currently suggests that raw or partially cooked eggs should not be given to babies or toddlers – so just to be on the safe side it's probably best to stick with well-cooked eggs only until your child is at school.

A bit of care is needed when buying and cooking with eggs too – especially where children are concerned. Follow this guide:

1   At home, always keep eggs in their box, in a cold refrigerator (5°C or below).
2   Wash hands before and after handling eggs to prevent cross contamination.
3   Eat eggs as close to the packing date as possible and certainly within the 'best before date' – use the date on the egg as a guide to freshness. Don't test freshness by putting eggs in a bowl of water.
4   Don't wash eggs because this makes them porous and can let bacteria inside.
5   Don't use cracked or dirty eggs.

The ideal breakfast food, try tempting your child away from toast and cereal occasionally with a hard boiled egg with a face drawn on it and some wholegrain toast soldiers.

Here's an idea for you... **Columbus Omega-3 rich eggs are sold in most large supermarkets and come from chickens that are fed on Omega-3 polyunsaturated fatty acid-enriched feed. Omega 3 is a type of 'essential' polyunsaturated fat which is thought to help maintain a healthy heart – it is also thought to be involved in keeping joints supple and is a vital building block for the brain. If your kids hate oily fish (one of the best sources of Omega 3) – these could be worth a go.**

'Egg in a cup' is another fun way to serve egg for breakfast or as a snack. Grease the inside of a cute china teacup or ramekin, break an egg into it and stand the cup in simmering water (the water should come half way up) for 8 minutes or so until the egg is cooked through. Allow the cup to cool before handing it over with a teaspoon.

For a meal at any time of day try the following.

MICROWAVE OMELETTE (SERVES 1–2)

Beat together 2 eggs, 1 tsp water, and add pepper to taste. Place 1 tbsp of butter in an 18cm non-metallic pie dish and melt in the microwave on a high setting for 30 seconds. Pour in the egg mixture, and stand the pie dish on an upturned plate in the microwave and cook on a medium-high setting for 1 minute. Use a fork to draw the outside of the cooked egg into the centre of the dish and microwave on a medium setting for a further 2 minutes. Stand for 1 minute before serving.

Before your omelette is set, add your favourite filling such as cheese, ham, steamed broccoli, mushrooms, tomatoes or even chicken tikka slices.

TORTILLA (SERVES 4–6)

This tea time treat is also great cold, in packed lunches.

To find out how to conjure up other quick meals with very little effort read IDEA 27, *Miracle meals.*

Try another idea...

Heat a tablespoon of oil in a frying pan, add a crushed garlic clove and 2 finely sliced onions and cook over a medium heat until soft. Meanwhile, peel and boil a medium-sized potato until cooked through, drain and then dice into bitesized pieces. Beat 6 large eggs in a bowl and stir in the onions and garlic, diced potato, a small can of sweetcorn, a handful of frozen peas and a handful of chopped chorizo or cooked bacon pieces. Pour the egg mixture back into the still-oily pan and cook over a medium heat for 5–10 minutes until set (draw the cooked edges of the tortilla into the centre with a wooden spoon or spatula for the first minute – then leave alone). Cut into slices.

And if you're child hates eggs – hide them in other recipes such as ...

PANCAKES

To make six pancakes, whisk together 50g/2oz plain flour and 1 egg, then slowly whisk in

'Love and eggs are best when they are fresh.'
Russian proverb

Defining idea...

¼ pint/150ml semi-skimmed milk to make a lump-free batter. Grease a frying pan with a little butter, and when smoking hot – pour in enough batter to cover the base of the pan. Once the pancake is cooked on one side, flip it and cook on the other. Remove and use as a 'wrap' filled with cheese, ham and salad or serve with fresh fruit.

How did it go?

Q   Eggs have quite a high cholesterol content, don't they – is that bad for health?

A   *It used to be thought that cholesterol in food was bad for our blood choles-terol levels – however, thanks to more recent research, we now know the cholesterol in food has little effect on blood cholesterol levels. What really affects blood cholesterol is the amount of saturated fat we eat in foods like fatty meats, full fat milk, butter, lard, cream, pastry, cakes and biscuits.*

Q   Is there a limit to the number of eggs that should be eaten in a week?

A   *No. Although there is no official upper limit recommended for the number of eggs anyone should eat a week, most nutritionists agree that eating two to four eggs a week is fine as part of a healthy, balanced diet.*

39
Little dippers

Children love to eat with their fingers – so dips will always make a popular snack, light lunch or dessert choice.

In fact, a bowl of dip and some crudités is a great way to tempt even the most veg-phobic child to munch on carrot batons, cucumber and baby sweetcorn.

Of course, there are a host of ready-made savoury dips around, but unfortunately many are high in fat, salt, artificial flavourings and preservatives. If you want to be absolutely sure that your child is getting the best then whizz up your own in a blender. The following taste so good that they'll go down equally well at a grown up drinks party.

SAVOURY SUCCESS

These savoury dips will all work well with a selection of bread sticks, mini pittas and vegetable crudités. Choose from: carrots, celery, red and yellow peppers, small boiled new potatoes, lightly steamed green beans, baby corn, sugar snap peas, small cauliflower florets and raw button mushrooms.

- Hummus. A beige dip made from chick peas does not sound promising – yet a surprising number of kids absolutely adore this Middle Eastern dip.

  Throw a tin of drained chickpeas, 2 crushed garlic cloves, 2 tablespoons of tahini paste (a sesame seed paste available from health food stores and supermarkets), 4 tablespoons of olive oil, and the juice of two lemons into a blender and blitz until smooth. Season with a little paprika and black pepper – and sprinkle paprika on top to decorate.

- Guacamole is another family favourite – and again, super-easy to make. This mild, child-friendly version uses sweet red pepper instead of the traditional chilli. Eat immediately, as avocado tends to discolour quite quickly.

  Place 2 ripe avocados (peeled and stone removed), 2 large ripe tomatoes (deseeded and chopped), a small chopped red onion, a garlic clove, ½ a red pepper and a good squeeze of lemon juice in a blender – and roughly chop – leaving the texture chunky. For extra fire add Tabasco sauce to taste.

- Tuna dip is a great way to get kids to eat more fish.

  Blend 110g/4oz tuna in spring water (drained) with a garlic clove, 2 tablespoons of olive oil, the juice of a lemon, 2 tablespoons Greek yogurt. Add pepper to taste. Stir in a tablespoon of capers for more sophisticated palates.

- Apple dip has just the right balance of sweet and savoury for children.

  Blend together a 250g pack of soft, low fat cream cheese, 3 tablespoons of low fat mayonnaise, a tablespoon of lemon juice and 2 peeled and chopped apples. Add chopped walnuts for an adult version of this dip.

Here's an idea for you... **Older children will enjoy using fondue forks or wooden barbecue skewers to spear their fruit and veg. If you can get hold of them, plastic, ornamental cocktail sticks or those little wooden forks you get in fish and chip shops also help to make dipping fun.**

SWEET TREATS

A sweet dip makes a fun, shared dessert for the family or when friends stay for tea. Serve with fresh fruit such as strawberries, bananas, grapes or firm cubes of melon, apple, nectarine, pear or peach. If you're feeling really indulgent, you can also use thin, plain biscuits such as langues de chat, ice cream wafers, crisp sponge trifle fingers or marshmallows to dip.

For more great snack food suggestions check out IDEA 14, Snack attack.

Try another idea...

- Greek yogurt. A pot of half fat Greek yogurt, fromage frais or creme fraiche with a swirl of fruit purée *or* lemon curd *or* honey and chopped toasted almonds (NB nuts should not be given to children under the age of five) makes an ideal light, summer dip.
- Caramel dip. Super sweet, but great with banana slices and apple cubes – simmer a large, unopened can of condensed milk in a saucepan of water over a low heat for 1 hour (the water should be halfway up the can – so check and top up water levels). Remove the can from the pan extremely carefully and leave to cool for at last 20 minutes before opening and decanting the delicious toffee-coloured caramel inside.
- Chocolate. Place a small pot of double cream and 100g/3½ oz milk chocolate, broken into squares, into a saucepan. Heat very gently – stirring occasionally until all the chocolate has melted and combined with the cream (do not allow to boil). Pour the warm sauce into a cool bowl to serve.

'You don't have to cook fancy or complicated masterpieces – just good food from fresh ingredients.'

JULIA CHILD, America's first lady of TV cooking, (1912–2004)

Defining idea...

171

How did it go?

Q   **We love dips in our house, and I can't wait to try making my own – but just one question. I usually serve our dips with tortilla chips or crisps – is there a reason for not mentioning our favourite snacks?**

A   *Tortilla chips and crisps are often extremely salty – and frequently contain artificial flavours. Many crisps are also very high in fat. Whilst these types of snack foods are OK in moderation, it's always a good idea to encourage your children to eat more healthy alternatives.*

Q   **But I'm not sure the kids will make the leap from tortilla chips to button mushrooms and cauliflower florets that easily. How can I persuade them?**

A   *Serve some less salty, carb-based dippers such as bread sticks and pitta bread alongside the vegetable crudités then. You can even make your own healthy tortilla chips by slicing soft flour tortillas into strips or triangles and placing them on a baking tray in a moderate oven for 10 minutes (don't let them turn brown). Leave to cool and go crisp before eating.*

Q   **I don't mean to be pedantic, but if healthy eating is so important why have you suggested chocolate and caramel dips in the sweet section?**

A   *Well, hopefully you'll serve the sweet dips with fresh fruit – and not every night, of course. As I said, everything is OK in moderation. They're fun desserts for special occasions.*

40

Takeaway tricks

Takeaways can easily fit into your child's lifestyle as an occasional meal as long as you choose some of the more healthy choices on offer.

Let's face it — there are times when only fast food or a takeaway will do.

Variety is really important when it comes to diet, so it's absolutely fine to have the odd burger and takeaway if the rest of what your child is eating is well balanced.

If you're paying a visit to a burger bar or having a Chinese for supper, the healthiest thing to do is to try and counterbalance your child's diet (and yours!) for the rest of that day. For example, if she's had a particularly salty meal – make an extra effort to ensure everything else that day is as low in salt as possible. If the meal had a high fat content – choose lower fat options for her other meals and snacks.

A common sense, balanced family approach to diet and lifestyle – i.e. regular sized chips rather than supersize, milk or fruit juice instead of fizzy pop, a game of football in the park rather than an afternoon in front of the TV – is also a great investment. It's a good idea to teach even small children to make healthier choices and

Here's an idea for you...

Don't be fooled by healthy sounding fish or veggie burgers – some of them contain more saturated fat than beef burgers. Many of the fast food and restaurant chains now provide detailed nutritional information on all their meals. Ask for a leaflet in the restaurant or log on to their website to find out which foods are best choices for you and your children. Both the McDonalds (www.mcdonalds.co.uk) and Burger King) www.burgerking.co.uk) websites have really useful functions where you can compare different items on the menu and find the nutritional totals for various meal combinations.

learn portion control, as food preferences and good eating habits are often established during this early stage of life.

TAKE IT AWAY

Burger bar

Sizes – like jumbo, super, giant and deluxe are best avoided in burger bars – or any other kind of fast food joint for that matter. Choose a regular sized hamburger with no cheese for preference.

A regular portion of chips is fine, just ask for them unsalted if possible. For a drink choose 100% fruit juice, milk or water. Skip the milkshakes and sugared fizzy drinks, particularly if she wants a dessert.

Fruit salad is a better choice for dessert than creamy ice cream or apple pie.

Fried chicken

Deep frying food more than doubles the amount of fat it contains. A piece of grilled chicken, for example, contains just 5.4g of fat compared to the 12.7g of fat contained in the same quantity of deep fried chicken. So try to persuade your kids to choose grilled chicken in their burger – especially if they're having chips as well.

Saying no to mayonnaise in a chicken sandwich can knock off up to 6.5g fat.

Saturated, unsaturated? Confused about fats? Read IDEA 26, *Get the right fatitude.*

Try another idea...

Indian

It's not the meat, it's the sauces that are the problem here – they can be loaded with fat. Try dishes baked in the Tandoor oven, like chicken tikka, tandoori or shashlik that come without a sauce. If you can't avoid creamy sauces like korma and tikka masala, which can contain a huge 47g of fat, according to one recent report – be frugal with the amount of sauce you spoon over the meat. The healthiest solution is to go for something tomato-based or with vegetables, like a rogan josh, and eat it with plain boiled rice. Think again before you order 'extras' too – poppadoms, samosas and bhajis are loaded with saturated fat.

Chinese

Again, avoid ordering too many deep fried, batter-covered dishes and those that are covered in sticky, sweet sauce, like pork balls and sweet and sour. Stir fries and boiled or steamed rice or noodles are good choices.

Pizza

If you want to have pizza – go for a thin crust with a basic topping, rather than the cheese-stuffed crust one that's piled high with meat and five different cheeses. Watch out for garlic bread – just one portion can contain more fat and calories than the average main meal. And take care with side salads.

'As a rule, children dislike foods which are said to be good for them, or are forced on them, and they take strong fancies to foods which they are not allowed to eat; advantage should be taken of these tendencies.'
    ERIC PRITCHARD, author of *Infant Education* (1907)

Defining idea...

175

Fish and chip shop

Let's face it – you're there to buy chips, so ideally make whatever you have with them as healthy as possible. Sausage in batter or a meat pie are not good choices, but cod and mushy peas is better, particularly if you don't eat all the batter. Roast chicken too is a relatively healthy choice if your kids hate fish.

How did it go?

Q   We like Thai food. That's a better choice than fish and chips isn't it?

A   *Thai meals generally contain steamed rice, fish and vegetables, and dishes are individually cooked, so this can be a pretty healthy takeaway. Watch out for the creamy sauces, however – a Thai green curry with sticky rice can contain 29g of fat.*

Q   We also like to go to our local Italian restaurant – what's the best choice there?

A   *Pasta is best served with a tomato-based or vegetable sauce, instead of a creamy or cheesy choice. Think tomato and basil rather than carbonara or lasagne. Grilled meat and fish dishes are often on the menu and can make a healthy meal with salad or vegetables.*

41

On the rack

Clever use of herbs and spices can make healthy meals child-friendly.

Just because a dish is healthy, however, doesn't mean it has to be bland and tasteless. Keep a small library of herbs, spices and flavourings and use them with abandon.

If you don't know where to start, the following list will give you some ideas for using common herbs and spices. Fresh herbs will generally give you the best result – but for practical reasons you may prefer to keep a selection of dried flavourings.

HERBS

Basil

Dried basil is OK, but fresh is better – grow your own or buy it in pots from the supermarket. Basil loses its flavour on cooking, so use it raw or add it to dishes at the last minute. It tastes great with pasta, pizza, tomatoes, Mediterranean vegetables; delicate cheeses, such as Mozzarella or Ricotta; garlic and lemon; potatoes and rice.

Bay

Dried bay leaves have a more intense and less bitter flavour than fresh. Bay leaves should be infused in a dish, then removed rather than eaten. Tear a few leaves to release the oils and add to slow-cooked stews, casseroles, soups or meat sauces. Alternatively skewer individual leaves between cubes of meat on kebabs before barbecuing, or tuck it into slashes on fish before baking.

Chives

Chives have a mild onion flavour and are best eaten raw. Snip them finely with scissors into anything eggy (think scrambled, and sandwiches), smoked fish; beetroot, carrots and other sweetish root vegetables. Chives are particularly good mixed with sour cream or cottage cheese to top baked potatoes or stirred into boiled potatoes and mayonnaise to make potato salad.

Dill

Use fresh dill raw, snipping or slicing the fronds roughly over cream cheese or smoked salmon. Stuff lots of dill into trout or sardines before baking in foil.

Mint

Bright and refreshing, mint is an incredibly versatile herb.

Here's an idea for you... **Scan the herb and spice section for themed, ready-mixed pastes, stir-fry blends and seasoning mixtures. You'll be able to make an impressive Thai stir fry, chicken fajitas or authentic bolognese without having to buy an armful of herbs and spices.**

178

Add sprigs to the cooking water for boiled potatoes, peas and carrots. A little shredded mint also tastes great with strawberries, apples, mangoes and melon.

For more ideas for adventurous eaters read IDEA 50, *Petits gourmets*.

Try another idea…

Oregano

The 'Italian' herb. Use dried oregano liberally in tomato-based pasta sauces, on pizza and in mozzarella and tomato sandwiches (drizzle with a little olive oil rather than using butter).

Parsley

Packed with vitamin C – fresh parsley tastes great sprinkled or stirred into just about anything. Use curly leaf for traditional British dishes and the flat leaf version for everything else. Good sprinkled over carrots, squash, parsnips or any sweet veg; crab and other shellfish; garlic and lemon; pork and ham. It also works well with carbs like pasta, couscous and rice.

Rosemary

A kitchen must-have. Strip the needles from the stems and chop them. If you're using rosemary to season roast veg, mix it into the roasting oil to stop it burning. Tastes fabulous with roast potatoes; garlic; lamb, chicken and pulses. It goes very well with honey too. Use the two together to make delicious marinades and glazes for grilled or barbecued meats.

'Tomatoes and oregano make it Italian; wine and tarragon make it French. Sour cream makes it Russian; lemon and cinnamon make it Greek. Soy sauce makes it Chinese; garlic makes it good.'

Defining idea…

ALICE MAY BROCK, American restaurant owner made famous by the Arlo Guthrie song and film 'Alice's Restaurant'

179

Sage

Strip the leaves from the stalks and cook, rather than using raw. It's a powerful flavour, so use with restraint. Tastes great with root vegetables, squashes and pork and is brilliant with a little butter and parmesan as a dressing for filled pasta like ravioli or even the plain, boiled variety.

Thyme

Ideal for stews because it keeps its flavour – pull the leaves from the woody stem and add to beef and lamb dishes and roast chicken. Lemon thyme tastes good sprinkled over fish.

SPICES

Cinnamon

A brilliant spice for adding flavour to fruit, cakes, biscuits and puddings. Use the powdered variety for economy and speed with baked bananas, stewed fruit and yogurt or rice pudding. It also goes well with rice, beef, pork, spinach and curries.

Garlic

Kids love it – and you can add it to most savoury dishes. Make bruschetta by rubbing a cut clove onto toast then topping it with finely chopped tomatoes sprinkled with a little olive oil and oregano. Alternatively try a little crushed garlic in Yorkshire pudding batter – yum!

Paprika

A good way to add a sweet, peppery flavour without the heat you get from chilli. Tastes great in winter stews and cheese and egg dishes.

Turmeric

As useful for its bright yellow colour as its earthy fragrance. Good for flavouring curries, potatoes and rice. Sprinkle it in cooking water to make 'gold' rice.

Q   We love garlic, but I find I waste a lot of fresh bulbs because they've gone dry or sprouted by the time I get round to using them. Any suggestions?

How did it go?

A   Real garlic obviously tastes best, but there are some good garlic paste alternatives in jars and tubes that you can use. Alternatively use garlic oil to flavour dishes.

Q   Can I make my own garlic oil?

A   It's best to buy ready-made. The Food Standards Agency say it's not a good idea to make flavoured oils at home unless you are going to use them immediately. Plants, including herbs and spices, can carry spores produced by the bacteria Clostridium botulinum, *which can cause botulism. Although rare,* Clostridium botulinum *multiplies in places without any oxygen, so if there are spores on your garlic cloves, putting them in oil can create the right conditions. Companies that produce flavoured oils formulate their products to make sure that this type of bacteria doesn't multiply – sorry!*

181

42

Chocs away!

Sticky, messy and delicious – your child will enjoy helping you make these simple chocolate treats as much as you both will enjoy eating them.

It is consistently voted the number one favourite food by children, so even the healthiest diet has to find room for a little chocolate now and again.

CHOCOLATE REFRIGERATOR CAKE (MAKES 8 SLICES)

All children will love pounding the biscuits for this simple, no-cook recipe.

Line a 1lb loaf tin with lightly greased foil. Place 350g/12oz digestive biscuits (this also works well with Ginger Nuts) in a plastic bag and bash with a rolling pin until you have a bag of small pieces and crumbs. Tip the crumbs and 50g/2oz dried fruit (glace cherries, raisins, chopped apricots, pears or chopped dates work well) into a mixing bowl. Melt 110g/4oz plain chocolate, 110g/4oz butter and 1 rounded table-spoon of golden syrup in a pan or microwave – then stir into the dry ingredients until all crumbs are coated with chocolate. Tip the mixture into the lined tin and press down firmly with the back of a spoon. Refrigerate overnight, before turning out, removing the foil and slicing.

WHITE CHOCOLATE BROWNIES (MAKES AROUND 20 BROWNIES)

A delicious twist on the traditional brownie.

Preheat your oven to 190°C/375°F/Gas 5. Line a 30cm × 20cm/12″ × 8″ Swiss roll tin or similar with lightly greased aluminium foil. Gently melt 125g/4½oz good quality white chocolate and 100g/3½ oz unsalted butter in a pan or microwave – then stir in 275g/10oz caster sugar until really well mixed. Add three large eggs – one at a time – then 1 tsp vanilla extract and 225g/8oz white chocolate chips (also 110g/4oz chopped hazelnuts if you're making these for adults). Next, stir in thoroughly 175g/6oz self raising flour and a pinch of salt and pour batter into the prepared tin. Bake for 30–35 minutes in the centre of the oven – then test. Unlike a conventional sponge, the centre should be only just starting to firm up. Cook it too long and you'll lose the fudgy texture. Allow to cool and set in the tray before turning out, removing foil and slicing into squares.

Here's an idea for you... **Everyone loves chocolate Rice Krispie cakes. So why not give yours a twist? Just fool around with the basic recipe. (Melt 125g/4½oz chocolate in a small basin over hot water, then stir in 50g/2oz Krispies. Drop spoonfuls of the mixture into cake cases and chill until firm.) For variation use white chocolate, chocolate orange or even mint chocolate in place of the milk. Along with the cereal – which, of course, could be Corn Flakes, Bran Flakes with sultanas or even Shreddies – stir in a couple of tablespoons of raisins, chopped apricot, coconut, M&Ms or tiny marshmallows.**

CHOCOLATE PIZZA (SERVES 4-6)

Kids will enjoy piling up the ingredients on this sweet treat.

Start with a ready-made pizza base. Preheat your oven as directed on the pizza base packaging then bake the base for just half the recommended time. In the meantime, mix together 125g/4oz cream cheese with 3 tbsps icing sugar and a tsp of vanilla extract until smooth. Spread cheese mixture over the hot

You'll find a recipe for
Chocolate Fondue in IDEA 39,
Little dippers.

Try another idea…

pizza base – leaving a 1cm/½" border around the edge then return to the oven for the remainder of the recommended baking time. Whilst pizza is still hot, sprinkle over a good handful of chocolate chips and allow them to melt – then add a layer of sliced fresh strawberries, a little whipped cream and chocolate sprinkles. (Serve immediately, or chill cheese and chocolate coated base before adding the strawberries and cream.)

CHOCOLATE CROISSANT PUDDING (SERVES 6)

This spin on bread and butter pudding is a great way to use up stale *pain au chocolat, brioche* – even chocolate or blueberry muffins.

Preheat the oven to 180°C/350°F/Gas 4 – then butter an ovenproof dish. Thickly slice four stale *pain au chocolat* or six muffins and lay the slices flat in the buttered dish. Whisk together 500ml/18fl oz double cream and 500ml/18fl oz semi-skimmed milk, four large eggs, 3 tbsps caster sugar and a teaspoon of vanilla extract – then pour liquid over the slices. Leave to soak 10 minutes – before baking for 30–40 minutes until golden.

'Never mind about 1066 William the Conqueror, 1087 William the Second. Such things are not going to affect one's life … but 1932 the (invention of the) Mars Bar and 1936 Maltesers and 1937 the Kit Kat – these dates are milestones in history and should be seared into the memory of every child in the country.'
ROALD DAHL, author of *Charlie and the Chocolate Factory*

Defining idea…

How did
it go?

Q   I tried to warm up the chocolate for the Rice Krispie cakes in a bowl over some boiling water – but instead of turning liquid it ended up as a thick lumpy mess. Why?

A   *Chocolate is very sensitive and can 'seize' for a couple of reasons. Firstly, you may have burned it. Chocolate needs a really, really low heat to melt – and plenty of stirring. When using the method you describe, do not let the water touch the bottom of the bowl that the chocolate is in. Secondly a small amount of moisture may have got into the chocolate – a damp spoon or drip of condensation is all it takes to ruin the batch.*

Q   Should I try melting the chocolate in the microwave then ...?

A   *Yes, but again, a light touch is essential for good results. Place chopped pieces of chocolate in a microwave-proof bowl and heat for just 30 seconds. Remove the bowl, stir what you can then return the bowl to the microwave for another 30 seconds and stir. Continue this method until the chocolate is almost melted then remove from the microwave and let the warmth of the bowl and surrounding chocolate complete the melting.*

43

Just desserts

A healthy diet doesn't mean pudding has to be off the menu. In fact, dessert is a great excuse to add extra fruit and other nutritious foods to your child's diet.

A little of what you fancy does you good, so it's better to be prepared with something that's both tasty and nutritious.

Pudding doesn't have to be an everyday event – but it's always handy to have those healthy choices available for days when your child just wants to eat … and eat…

No matter how nutritious that first course has been, it's best to avoid packet cakes, sweets or chocolate for everyday 'afters'. These types of ready-made desserts will all too quickly train your child to expect oversweetened, artificially flavoured foods – a habit that can be really difficult to break as he gets older.

You don't have to be a complete spoilsport, however – just make sure junk desserts are the exception rather than the rule, to be eaten at parties and at Granny's (who will, rest assured, have a cupboard full of the stuff – no matter what you tell her). If there's no junk in the house – he can't ask for it.

Here's an idea for you... **In warm weather – make your own fruit lollies. Lolly moulds can be bought cheaply from most major department stores and large supermarkets. Fill the moulds with fruit juice or fresh fruit purée (try strawberries, raspberries, kiwis or pineapple) and freeze for two hours. Experiment with exotic fruit cocktails or blend fruit with vanilla yogurt or banana for smoothies-on-a-stick. Stripy lollies look great too. Use two or three different fruit purées – allowing each layer to freeze for an hour before you add the next.**

Bribing children to eat a healthy main meal with the promise of a sticky pudding is an easy pitfall to fall into too. Avoid passing on the subconscious message that chicken and vegetables are just something to plough through before he gets to the yummy pudding – and never, never offer dessert if your child refuses to eat his main meal.

A healthy pud starts at the supermarket, so aim your trolley at the fruit section …

Fresh fruit desserts don't have to be boring.

■ *Fruit kebabs*, made by threading a variety of brightly coloured, bite-sized chunks of fruit onto wooden barbecue skewers are fun to eat. Cubes of apple, pear, melon, mango and pineapple, slices of banana, nectarine segments, strawberries and grapes all work well.

■ *Baked bananas* take seconds to prepare and can be chucked in the oven while the main course is cooking. Peel a banana and slice it in half lengthways. Place the two pieces on a large square of foil and top with a small smear of butter, a sprinkle of brown sugar and a pinch of cinnamon *or* a handful of raspberries and a tablespoon of orange juice, *or* lightly butter the foil and sandwich a small, grated square of chocolate or a little chocolate hazelnut spread between the slices. Wrap the banana and its topping up in the foil and bake at 180°C/350°F/Gas 4 for 15–20 minutes.

■ *Fruit set in jelly* always goes down well too – and it's super-cheap. Look for packs of real fruit juice jelly, follow the instructions for making it up, then add the fruit of your choice (NB fresh pineapple, kiwi and papaya contain enzymes that will prevent jelly from setting – so are best avoided).
Mandarin segments, grapes, raspberries, blueberries and strawberries will all do the trick.

■ *Oat-based fruit crumbles* make a really healthy winter pudding for the whole family (oats have been shown to help reduce cholesterol). For a dish to serve six, use a combination of fresh fruit – for example, four Bramley apples, peeled, cored and sliced, and a handful of blackberries *or* eight peaches, stoned and sliced with a handful of raspberries. Sprinkle the fruit with 2 tablespoons of brown sugar to sweeten. To make the crumble topping, rub 50g/2oz unsalted butter into 100g/3½oz oats. Sprinkle crumble over the fruit and bake in a preheated oven 230°C/430°F/Gas 8 until golden brown. Serve with a little custard, ice cream or half fat fromage frais.

If your child loves pots of flavoured yogurt and fromage frais – choose carefully. Many of the most popular brands are packed with sugar and additives. See IDEA 12, *Label conscious*, for a guide to reading food labels.

Try another idea...

'*The proof of the pudding is in the eating.*'
Proverb

Defining idea...

How did
it go?

Q **Buying a broad variety of fresh fruit for desserts is a great idea, but I find that I never get round to using it all. The sell by dates on punnets of raspberries and whole pineapples seem to whizz by in no time and the whole lot ends up in the bin. It's a real waste.**

A *I know exactly what you mean. Instead of buying vast quantities of exciting fresh fruit each week, try keeping a stock of frozen and dried fruit – and even fruit canned in fruit juice. Things like frozen fruits of the forest, canned cherries and dried mango strips all have a really long shelf life and are handy 'waste-free' ways to add variety to the family's fruit consumption.*

Q **So what I can do with all the fruit that's left in the bowl right now? The stuff that no one fancies eating?**

A *Very ripe fruit is often deliciously sweet – if not so lovely to look at. Most fruit can be peeled, then stewed with a little water to make a compote (rough fruit purée). Just be sure to remove all pips and stones before cooking. Freeze compotes to use within the month or use immediately to top rice pudding, yogurt or ice cream. Old apples, pears and stone fruit such as mangoes, plums, peaches and apricots – and berries – can all be disguised in crumbles and pies. Citrus fruit, grapes and most other fruit, with the exception of bananas, are great candidates for the juicer – if you have one.*

44

Whizz it up

Nutritious and versatile, fruit smoothies and shakes make a super-healthy snack, or even a quick breakfast for reluctant eaters.

So dust off your blender and mix up a delicious, glassful of goodness in just 60 seconds.

Suitable for children of one year and over, smoothies and shakes really are a great way to bump up your child's daily fruit and/or dairy intake.

Making your own drinks – or allowing the kids to do their own – is really quick and easy too, and a great way to use up excess garden produce or pick-your-own fruit. Overripe fruit, fruit canned in its own juice and frozen fruit also work especially well in smoothies and shakes.

Experiment with your own combinations: try to balance tart and sweet fruit, and dense, fibre-rich fruit like bananas, mangoes and pineapple (which also add thickness), with watery fruit like strawberries, kiwi fruit and oranges.

Add runny yoghurt, milk or even a scoop of ice cream for creaminess and calcium, and crushed ice cubes for extra chill. If you are feeling creative, drop a little grated

Here's an idea for you… **For a super-chilled smoothie – put peeled, chopped bananas and washed berries in the freezer for a minimum of three hours before adding them to your blender.**

fresh ginger, cinnamon, mint or vanilla extract into the blender too. You may need to add a little honey for sweetness if your smoothie tastes too sharp for young palates.

Even though they are packed with protective antioxidant vitamins and dietary fibre, do be careful how and when you offer these delicious drinks, however. A filling shake or smoothie too close to meal times will dull your child's appetite – and more than one fruit-based drink a day could lead to diarrhoea

The following recipes all provide one serving. In every case, wash fruit and keep the skin on where appropriate – but do remove cores, seeds and stones. Serve immediately, as smoothies have a tendency to separate.

YOU'RE SO SMOOTH

Rise and shine

Packed with vitamin C, this smoothie is ideal for breakfast time – and for banishing adult hangovers. If it tastes too sharp, add a teaspoon of honey.

Blend together a big handful of fresh strawberries, hulled, 150ml/¼ pint orange juice and one kiwi fruit, peeled and cores removed.

Passion fruit and pear refresher

The combination of delicate pear juice and powerful passion fruit and raspberry makes an unusual, refreshing drink.

Blend a large, chopped banana, the scooped out flesh from one passion fruit and eight raspberries with the juice from two pears (if you have a juicer) – or 150ml/¼ pint ready-made pear juice.

Try another idea...

Want to make up your own smoothie recipes? Read IDEA 16, *Get fruity*, for an inspiring guide to a more interesting fruit bowl.

Blueberry buzz

Berries contain some of the highest levels of antioxidants around – they are also packed with fibre.

Wash a small punnet of blueberries (raspberries, blackberries and strawberries will also work well here if you prefer) and blend with a large, chopped banana – then add 150ml/¼ pint unset, low fat natural yogurt and blitz ingredients together quickly.

Tropical treat

This filling recipe will work equally well with papaya or mango.

Blend together a large banana, the flesh of half a large mango, the juice of ½ lime and 150ml/¼ pint apple juice.

Melon miracle

A delicately flavoured blend – great for breakfast or elevenses on a warm day.

Defining idea...

'Do not allow children to mix drinks. It is unseemly and they use too much vermouth.'
STEVE ALLEN (1921–2000), American comedian

Blend together a big handful each of chopped, deseeded watermelon and chopped honeydew melon, juice of ½ a lime, a small pot of vanilla yogurt and a handful of crushed ice.

Peanut butter smoothie

Packed with energy – this is naughty – but nice (and obviously unsuitable for anyone with a nut allergy).

Blend together a scoop of vanilla or chocolate ice cream, 150ml/¼ pint semi-skimmed milk and 2 tablespoons of peanut butter (it also tastes great if you add a banana to the recipe).

Banana-berry milkshake

A meal in a glass – or a summer bedtime drink.

Blend a banana and a handful of sliced strawberries, frozen fruits of the forest or raspberries with 150ml/¼ pint semi-skimmed milk, a tablespoon of natural yogurt and a teaspoon of honey.

Papaya milkshake

According to the Chinese, this drink is great for the skin and digestion.

Blend together the flesh (minus the seeds) of a half a papaya and 150ml/¼ pint semi-skimmed milk. Add a teaspoon or two of sugar to taste.

Q **The smoothies and shakes taste great – but some of them are so thick, you could almost eat them with a spoon. Is that how a smoothie should be – or am I doing something wrong?**

How did it go?

A *You're doing everything right – smoothies are supposed to have a thick consistency. If you like yours more liquid, however, don't be afraid to add a little more fruit juice or ice to your concoction. For a delicious dessert you can also do the opposite, and add even more fruit chunks to the smoothie recipe to make a healthy purée that you can eat from bowls – with a spoon.*

Q **I've added some more fruit juice – unfortunately the drink is still too thick for the kids to drink it through a straw. They use their fingers to try and get the really tasty bit that gets left at the bottom of a long glass. It drives me mad! Any tips on smoothie etiquette?**

A *A straw is always a good idea with a smoothie, or a milkshake – but you're right, the average straw is just too narrow. You can buy packs of wide-bore 'Slush Straws' or Spoon Straws (wide straws with a spoon-like lip at the bottom for scraping out the last bits) from cook shops, or try on the web – www.barmans.co.uk or www.penineteaandcoffee.co.uk.*

   Alternatively, get them to sip their smoothie and supply a long handled ice cream spoon to reach the dregs.

45
Little chefs

Teaching your child to cook is one of the very best ways to encourage him to adopt healthy eating habits.

So, whatever his age, encourage your child to join you in the kitchen.

Cooking is a wonderful way to teach your child about a huge range of subjects. Encouraging him to taste as he goes will help his powers of description and make him braver about trying new foods. Cooking teaches planning and organisation, kitchen safety and hygiene. All that weighing and measuring can introduce basic mathematical concepts and creating a dish himself will nurture his artistic side too. Older children may even learn something about other cultures and geography as you create, say, an Italian- or Indian-influenced meal.

So let's get started …

- Tie back long hair, roll up loose sleeves and wear something that's OK to get messy.
- Wash hands.
- Keep a damp cloth or paper towel nearby to wipe up spills.
- Begin by reading through your chosen recipe from start to finish to make sure you understand exactly what you'll need to do – older children can do this with you.

Here's an idea for you…

Home-made lemonade is just the thing for a hot, sunny day. Slice in half then juice 4 lemons (remove any pips as you go). Mix the lemon juice and 100g/3½ oz caster sugar together in a large jug until the sugar is dissolved. Add handfuls of ice to the jug, then 1 litre/2 pints of sparkling mineral water. Give it all a good stir and serve.

■ Make sure you have all your ingredients and all the necessary equipment to hand before you start.

■ Let your child help measure out the ingredients. Big kids can do this themselves – but young ones will enjoy the measuring jug, scales and counting spoonfuls. Make sure the ingredients get measured out accurately.

■ Observe all the usual kitchen safety rules while you're cooking – paying particular attention to hot surfaces, pans and electrical equipment. Never leave a young child alone in the kitchen.

■ And finally … make him help with the clearing up!

There are lots of simple recipes that you can make with your child throughout this book – but you can't go wrong if you start with one of these three.

SIMPLE FLAPJACKS (MAKES 8–12 FLAPJACKS)

Quick and easy to make – your child can pop one of these in his lunch box.

Preheat the oven to 180°C/350°F/Gas 4. Grease a shallow Victoria sponge tin with a little butter. Put 100g/3½ oz butter, 2 tablespoons of golden syrup and 2 tablespoons of Demerara sugar in a saucepan and melt on a very low heat. Take the pan off the heat and stir in 150g/5oz porridge oats – mixing well. Tip the mixture into the tin and press down with the back of a spoon. Bake in centre of the oven for 20 minutes or until golden brown. Remove tin from the oven and allow to cool for 15 minutes before scoring into wedges. Leave flapjack in tin until completely cold.

Fairy cakes are easy to make and fun to share. Find the recipe in IDEA 46, *Party on.*

Try another idea…

EASY PIZZAS (MAKES 4 SMALL PIZZAS)

Preheat the oven to 180°C/350°F/Gas 4. Lightly grease a baking sheet. Sieve 225g/8oz self raising flour into a bowl, then pour in 100ml/4 fl oz milk and 55ml/2 fl oz olive oil – mix with a fork to make a dough. Lightly flour a work surface, tip out the dough and knead lightly until smooth. Divide the dough into quarters. Roll each piece into a ball then flatten with hands to make 4 pizza bases approx 10cm/4" across. Place the bases on the baking sheet. Spread a tablespoon of passata (sieved tomatoes) on each base, then top with the ingredients of your choice: strips of ham and sliced mushrooms; tuna and thinly sliced onion rings; salami and thinly sliced red pepper. Grate over some cheddar cheese and bake for 10 minutes until golden. Allow to cool a little before eating.

QUICK QUICHE (SERVES 6)

Let your child cook this one for the whole family. He can make his own pastry once he gains confidence.

Defining idea…

Preheat the oven to 180°C/350°F/Gas 4. Roll out a pack of ready-made short crust pastry to line a 20cm diameter, 4cm deep flan tin. Prick the pastry with a fork, cover with foil and fill with baking beans. Bake for 10 minutes then remove the foil and beans and bake for a fur-

'In the childhood memories of every good cook, there's a large kitchen, a warm stove, a simmering pot and a mom.' (or dad)

BARBARA COSTIKYAN,
New York food critic

ther 10 minutes. Remove the pastry from the oven and turn down to 170°C/325°F/ Gas 3. Meanwhile, fry 125g/4½ oz cubed pancetta or bacon until crisp and drain any fat. Whisk together four egg yolks and three whole eggs. Stir in 400ml creme fraiche, 3 tbsps snipped chives and some grated nutmeg. Spread the bacon over the pastry base, then pour in the egg mixture. Cook for 30–40 minutes until set. Serve warm or cold with salad or roast vegetables.

How did it go?

Q   I can't drag my twins away from their computer games. Any tips for getting them into the kitchen?

A   *Next time you go shopping allow them to choose some ingredients to create a dish with. Perhaps they could look for their own pizza toppings or fillings for a quiche. The secret is to let them get really involved. Don't warn them off certain tasks because they'll make a mess – let them get engrossed.*

Q   I'm not sure it will work – they hate the supermarket. What else can I do?

A   *Invest in a gaudy selection of cake decorating toppings – think squeezy icing pens, silver balls, sugar flowers etc. and suggest you make fairy cakes and ice them. They'll definitely join in – because all kids love eating the baubles as they decorate.*

46

Party on

Catering for a children's party really doesn't have to be a parent's worst nightmare.

Forget about healthy eating rules for the day and keep things simple, however, and you will be able to enjoy the day as much as your child and her guests.

The following guidelines can be applied to any party you throw for a young child and will ensure you have the whole thing under control from the word go.

SANDWICHES – THE SAVOURY STAPLE

If you don't want to be left with a heap of opened and discarded sandwiches, there are four basic rules to follow:

- Don't try to be inventive with the fillings.
- Don't give the children too much choice.
- Don't overfill the sandwiches.
- Don't put salad in them.

Most children simply won't be impressed with Coronation chicken or prawns, and slices of cucumber or tomato are, sadly, guaranteed to put them off.

Here's an idea for you...

Individual cardboard party food boxes come in the shape of everything from Princess carriages to pirate ships – with slots for sandwiches, crisps and cakes. They're not cheap, but one of the best ways to keep party food mess to a minimum – and avoid over catering. Alternatively buy decorated cellophane bags and fill with individual party treats. Log on to www.partytreasures.co.uk or www.partybox.co.uk for ideas.

Pick two of the following simple fillings: ham, cheese, Marmite, turkey or chicken slices and put them between medium or thin-cut slices of bread. To avoid arguments I would stick to one type of bread too, rather than providing white and wholemeal versions of everything.

I know it sounds really boring, but believe me – particularly with younger children – this is what they like and what works best. If you want to dress up your sandwiches, the only thing you should do is put them on interesting plates.

OTHER SAVOURY STUFF

Oh, they're so predictable – but children love mini sausages. Buy good quality ones and lots of them. Serve warm if possible.

When it comes to crisps and so on – again, don't go crazy with lots of choices and exotic flavours. Children like the familiar and the simple. One, or maximum two, types of crisps or potato shapes are fine. I find a big plastic tumbler of breadsticks always goes down well too – even with older children.

FRUIT AND VEG

I always put a bowl of sliced, bite-sized fruit and veg on the table too – and it does get eaten. Think carrot, celery and cucumber batons, cherry tomatoes, grapes and

strawberries (slice grapes, tomatoes and strawberries as they are easy to choke on).

WHAT THEY'RE REALLY AFTER …

The sugary stuff, of course, is what all kids
want to eat at a party. If it's a hot day, or the
party is being held in your house, I would
veer away from anything coated in chocolate
– unless you want to be wiping up sticky hand prints for the rest of the year. For
similar reasons avoid anything in a wrapper.

Instead go for a plate of small-sized, brightly iced biscuits, and/or the sort with jam in
the middle, and/or mini gingerbread men. Also one or two types of cake – depending on whether you are serving the birthday cake at the party, or it's being taken
home. French fancies, mini muffins and brightly topped cup cakes all work well.

THE BIRTHDAY CAKE

You're probably going to hate me for saying this – but there's something about even
the most poorly executed, home-made birthday cake that beats the pants off any
best shop-bought version. My advice is, if you're going to make just one thing, let
it be the cake. I usually hire the appropriate number-shaped cake tin for my child's
age from my local cook shop. Make a Victoria sponge, sandwiched together with
vanilla butter cream (you can buy the ready-made stuff in a tub for convenience)
and jam. Top with a thin layer of warmed apri-
cot jam followed by ready-rolled royal icing,
which you simply drape over the cake and

Try another idea…

**Make a batch of iced biscuits
or brightly iced fairy cakes,
in place of one of the shop-
bought items mentioned here
– read IDEA 47, *Here's one
I prepared earlier*, for easy
recipes if you're feeling like a
domestic goddess or god!**

Defining idea…

*'Birthdays are nature's way of
telling us to eat more cake.'*
Unknown author

203

trim. Decorate the cake with handmade marzipan characters if you're so inclined or go for plastic animals, dolls, sweets, sugar flowers and candles. Ice your child's name with a tube of brightly coloured writing icing from the cake-making section of your local supermarket.

How did it go?

Q   Erm, how do you make a Victoria sponge?

A   *It's really easy. This recipe works best if all the ingredients are at room temperature before you start. Preheat your oven to 180°C/350°F/Gas 4. Grease two Victoria sponge tins. Put 225g/8oz each soft unsalted butter, caster sugar and self raising flour, 1 tsp baking powder, 1 tsp vanilla extract and 4 large eggs in a food processor and blend until smooth. Whilst the mixture is still blending pour in up to 4 tablespoons of milk – adding them one at a time and stopping once the mixture is of a soft, dropping consistency. Bake for around 30 minutes in the middle of the oven until the cakes are firm and coming away from the sides of the tins.*

Q   My three-year-old's birthday is in November, so his party will have to be indoors. Any tips for stopping drinks getting spilt everywhere?

A   *I would provide drinks that come in cartons with a straw or the ones that come in ready-made drinking bottles. Alternatively you can buy cardboard cups with plastic lids and straws (like the ones you get in burger bars) online and from larger supermarkets and party shops.*

47

Here's one I prepared earlier

These super-easy biscuit and cake recipes guarantee effortless success.

Birthday parties, school fetes, picnics, Sunday tea, rainy afternoons stuck indoors with the kids ... some days just cry out for a bit of home baking.

Ok, so the bakes I recommend here may not be the most original in the world, but the good thing about them is they are really, really simple. So simple in fact, a child could make them – which is half of the idea really. Encouraging your child to bake is a great way to help him get interested in cooking.

FAIRY CAKES (MAKES 12 CAKES)

Make them pink and girly or decorate them with spider shapes – they'll all get eaten.

Preheat your oven to 200°C/400°F/Gas 6. Lay out 12 paper cake cases in a bun tin. Put 125g/4½ oz each of soft, unsalted butter, caster sugar and self raising flour in a food processor plus ½ tsp baking powder, 2 large eggs and a ½ teaspoon of vanilla

Use an icing nozzle or skewer to make a hole in the top of your gingerbread men or sugar cookies before they're baked. You can then thread them with ribbon once they're cooled – to hang on a Christmas tree, tie in bows or attach labels to.

extract (an additional big fistful of chocolate chips also works well here or try adding the grated zest of half a lemon or orange instead of the vanilla). Blitz until well blended, then add up to 3 tablespoons of milk – one at a time until the mix has a smooth dropping consistency. Spoon the mixture equally into all the paper cases and bake for 20 minutes. Remove the cakes and place on a wire rack to cool. Meanwhile, prepare the icing.

Icing

Make up half a packet of royal icing. When it's the right consistency, it should be stiff enough to create a reasonably thick layer on top of the cakes, and just runny enough to slump to a flat surface soon after it has been spread. Split the icing between two or three bowls if you want a selection of coloured toppings. Use food colouring – a tiny bit at a time – to get the right colours. (Paste colours which are available from specialist cook shops and online, are easy to use and give the best selection of colours.) Of course you can leave the icing white if you choose. Now decorate the tops as exuberantly as you wish – you know most kids will only eat the topping anyway. You can buy all kinds of decorations including mini chocolate beans, sugar flowers, marzipan animals, silver balls, hundreds and thousands and so on from your local supermarket.

SUGAR COOKIES (MAKES 8 BISCUITS)

Cut these to any shape you like – use your child's plasticine cutters if you don't have any interesting cookie cutters.

Preheat your oven to 190°C/375°F/Gas 5 and grease a baking sheet. Beat 100g/3½oz unsalted butter until soft. Add 100g/3½oz caster sugar and beat until light and fluffy. Gradually add one beaten egg, beating the mixture all the time. Add 275g/10oz plain flour and ½ tsp vanilla extract and mix well. Lift the ball of biscuit mix out and roll out on a floured surface until it's the same thickness as a £1 coin. Use cookie cutters to make shapes, then lift the uncooked biscuits onto the baking sheet with a fish slice. Bake the biscuits for 8–10 minutes until golden. Leave to harden on the baking sheet for a couple of minutes, then put on a wire rack to cool. Spread with icing (see icing instructions above) and decorate with sweets, writing icing or dried fruit.

To ensure your child's birthday party goes smoothly read IDEA 46, *Party on.*

Try another idea…

GINGERBREAD MEN (MAKES 12 BISCUITS)

Gingerbread men (or women) are a great bake for any occasion. Decorate them with iced outfits once they're cooked and cooled or simply press currants into the uncooked biscuits where the eyes, mouth and buttons should go before they go into the oven.

Preheat your oven to 190°C/375° F/Gas 5. Sift 350g/12oz plain flour, 1 tsp bicarbonate of soda and 2 tsps ground ginger into a food processor and add 110g/4oz cold butter cut into cubes. Blitz until the mixture resembles bread crumbs, then quickly stir in 175g/6oz soft, light brown sugar. In a bowl, beat together an egg and 4 tbsps golden syrup, then add to the dry mixture and blitz until it forms a dough. Knead the dough on a lightly floured surface until smooth then split it into two pieces. Roll out the first piece to 5mm/¼" thickness and use a gingerbread man, gingerbread woman or any

'Let them eat cake.'

Attributed to QUEEN MARIE ANTOINETTE (1755–1793)

Defining idea…

207

other cutter you fancy to cut the dough into biscuit shapes. Place them on lightly greased baking sheets and bake for 12 minutes or until golden. Leave to cool on the baking sheets for 2 minutes then transfer to a wire rack.

How did it go?

Q **I'd love to have a go at baking biscuits and cakes for my daughter's birthday party, but I always seem to run out of time just before the big event. Any tips?**

A *You can make the cookie and gingerbread dough anytime and freeze it for future use. Pack it as a fat, flattened disk in an airtight freezer bag and defrost thoroughly before you roll it out. You can also freeze the baked but undecorated fairy cakes in airtight boxes or bags.*

Q **How long will they keep in the freezer for?**

A *The biscuit dough should keep well for 2 months – the cakes for 4 months. Don't forget to write the date you put them in the freezer on the packaging, so you can keep track of how long they've been in there.*

48

The food pharmacy

Boost your family's immune systems with the right diet and lifestyle habits, and you might just manage to fight off some of the worst infections.

Sometimes it can seem as if children shake off one cough, cold or tummy upset, only to get another.

So, if you want your kids to be full of health and bounce, bear the following in mind.

- Make sure everyone is eating a well-balanced diet. See the chapter appropriate to your child's age group for more advice on this.
- Avoid foods that have exceeded their use by dates or seem to be past their prime – they may contain bacteria that can challenge the immune system.
- Lack of sleep leaves us more prone to infection – so put a bedtime routine in place now.
- Stress adversely affects the immune system – so encourage older children to share their worries and learn a few relaxation techniques.
- Regular exercise is important. Apart from boosting circulation and aerobic fitness, regular moderate exercise increases the number of NK (natural killer) cells in our bodies.
- Wash hands frequently and dry with disposable paper towels or freshly laundered towels. Many germs can be transmitted by physical contact. Washing

Better safe than sorry. If you are at all concerned about your child's health, always seek medical advice. Never be tempted to diagnose and treat a problem yourself.

hands frequently can significantly reduce the chances of catching the rotavirus too, which tends to infect children and causes vomiting and diarrhoea.

NUTRIENTS TO KEEP COLDS AT BAY

Vitamin C

Vitamin C has been shown to have the potential to prevent and also reduce the severity of the common cold. But before you reach for the supplements, consider upping the amount of vitamin C in your family's diet.

Fresh citrus fruits (such as orange, grapefruits, clementines, mandarins and lemons), kiwi fruit, strawberries, blackcurrants, dark green, leafy vegetables, red peppers and potatoes cooked in their skins are all good sources of vitamin C.

Vitamin C begins to be lost from the minute a fruit or vegetable is picked – so obviously the fresher you buy fruits and vegetables the better. Remember that frozen fruit and veg tends to have high levels of vitamin C as they are preserved as quickly as possible after picking. Eating produce raw or keeping cooking time to a minimum will also help to preserve vitamin C.

Zinc

Zinc plays an extremely important role in maintaining a healthy immune system too – if you are deficient in this mineral you are much more likely to catch a cold and to keep it for longer. Making sure your family's diet contains rich sources of zinc such as shellfish, lean meat, eggs, hard, crumbly cheeses like Parmesan, wholegrain products, nuts and seeds should help.

Magnesium

Magnesium has also been linked to a strong immune system – but again, there should be no need for supplements. A diet containing plenty of magnesium-rich foods such as green leafy vegetables, nuts and seeds, pulses and wholegrains should do the trick.

Storing and cooking foods safely is vital if you want to keep tummy upsets at bay. Read IDEA 2, *Keep it clean*, for important tips.

Try another idea...

NB Whole nuts should not be given to children under the age of five because of the danger of choking. Nut butters can be given from 12 months onwards, however. Shellfish are also best avoided until your child is at least 12 months old.

CONVALESCENCE

You've tried your best, but your child has come down with a cold. What next?

Many children who are feeling under the weather don't fancy much to eat – so it's best to go with their appetite. Make sure your child has plenty of fluids available to drink throughout the day and try to offer small portions of nutritious foods to tempt her.

I reckon being ill as one of the great pleasures of life, provided one is not too ill and is not obliged to work till one is better.
SAMUEL BUTLER, English satirist (1612–1680)

Defining idea...

According to research, chicken soup (or Jewish penicillin as it's sometimes known) really can help us recover when we've got a cold. Researchers recently discovered that home-made chicken soup could inhibit the migration of white blood cells which may cause bronchial congestion. The amino acid cysteine in chicken meat was shown to help thin mucus. The combination of the heat of the soup, the fats, herbs and water can also loosen thick mucus. Adding garlic also helps the soup's antiviral and antibacterial properties.

So if your child is tucked up on the settee with a cold – this might be just the thing to put some colour back in her cheeks.

CHICKEN SOUP (SERVES 6–8)

Bring 2.4 litres/4 pints chicken stock to the boil in a large saucepan. Then add approximately 1.35kg/3lbs lbs rinsed, raw, skinless chicken pieces (ideally, leave the bones in). Return to the boil, turn the heat right down and simmer very, very gently for 1 hour, uncovered. Now slice up the following and add: a large carrot, a large onion, 3 cloves of garlic, a stalk of celery, white and light green parts of a well-washed leek, a parsnip, a peeled sweet potato, a small peeled swede and a handful of fresh dill. Simmer for a further 30 minutes, stirring occasionally. Skim off any fat and season to taste before serving

How did it go?

Q **My son is always getting colds, probably because he refuses to eat fruit and vegetables – any tips?**

A *Fruit smoothies and juices, veggie juices (you can buy some really delicious, ready-made vegetable juice blends in the supermarket now, if you don't have a juicer) and vegetable soups can be a really useful way of getting your child to have more fruit and veg in his diet.*

Q **He'll drink fruit juices and smoothies, but I can't see him going for vegetable juice – and he hates soup.**

A *I would start blending a handful of steamed vegetables into his main meals where you can, then. Veggies can be made to 'disappear' in pasta sauces, stews, cottage pie and even gravy.*

49

Supersavers

Feeding your family does not have to be an expensive business.

If you're fed up with throwing away uneaten food that's passed its sell by date and dread those weekly shopping bills — read on.

This twelve step guide to clever shopping and crafty cooking may help to cut your food bills by as much as 20%.

1   *Make a proper shopping list.* Take some time to roughly plan your meals for the week and then write down what you need. Keep paper and a pencil in the kitchen, so you can write down items as you think of them. Check your kitchen cabinets and refrigerator as you make your list to be sure you're not doubling up on previous purchases.

2   *Shop once a week – and leave the kids at home.* Fewer trips to the shops mean fewer chances to load up on things you don't need. Shopping at quiet times and leaving the kids at home will give you time to think about what you're buying, check prices and look for bargains.

Can't decide what to cook tonight? Forget expensive cookery books, just visit a celebrity chef's website. All of the following have lots of great online recipes for you to try:
www.nigella.com
www.jamieoliver.net
www.deliaonline.com
www.nicknairncookschool.com
www.rivercottage.net
www.garyrhodes.com

3   *Beware the BOGOF!* 'Buy one, get one free' (BOGOF) and three for two offers are only good value if they are for products you would buy anyway. If you usually buy cheap, puffy corn crisp cereal, two for one super-duper muesli will still be more expensive – even if it's on offer. However, if your usual brand of loo roll, or similar non-perishable item, is on offer for three for two, buy as many as you can.

4   *Eyes down for a bargain.* Learn the tricks of the trade. Supermarkets often place expensive brands at eye level (the big manufacturers pay a premium to have their goods displayed on these shelves). The cheaper brands will usually be hiding on the lower levels.

5   *Buy in bulk.* The prices really are better when you buy in bulk – but watch out for the pitfalls. If you're not careful, you can end up spending a lot on items that you don't really need or food that whizzes past its sell-by date before you get round to using it. Here are a few tips:

- Make a list beforehand of things you use a lot of, such as baked beans or baby wipes. These are the perfect items to buy in bulk.
- Concentrate on non-perishable items. Kitchen roll can be stored in the garage – salmon steaks can't.
- Check the best before dates on food to be sure that it won't go off before you come to use it.

6 *Be seasonal.* Seasonal fruit and veg will always be cheaper than the 'just flown in from Kenya' sort. Adapt your cooking to accommodate seasonal foods and think about buying fresh produce from local markets rather than supermarkets. It will almost always be cheaper.

To find out more about storing food in your freezer turn to IDEA 51 – *The big freeze.*

Try another idea...

7 *Be loyal.* Sign up for a supermarket loyalty card – you'll be paid points for a certain percentage of your spending. It's a bit of a trade-off, but you will often receive personalised offers relating to products the supermarket knows you buy from the data it holds about your shopping habits.

8 *Get off your trolley.* If you're not going to the supermarket for a major shop, take a basket or small trolley at the door. Then, it's harder to overload with unnecessary items.

9 *Limit ready meals.* As a rule it's much cheaper to eat foods made from scratch than prepared foods. But use your common sense. Puréeing your own baby food may be much cheaper than buying it in jars, but if your little angel won't eat anything but his favourite brand, you'll be wasting time and money.

10 *Freeze please.* How many times have you put leftovers into the fridge and forgotten about them because you didn't fancy eating chicken two days in a row? Get in the habit of putting freshly cooked leftovers in the freezer (do not refreeze pre-cooked food like ready meals that have already been frozen once). That way you'll know they'll be ready to eat tomorrow or in two weeks.

11 *You must remember this.* Next time you cook – whether it be lasagne, soup or cake – double the amount, then freeze half of it.

'The most remarkable thing about my mother is that for 30 years she served the family nothing but leftovers. The **original** meal **has never been found.**'

CALVIN TRILLIN, American food writer

Defining idea...

215

12 *Go veggie.* The highest cost item on many people's shopping lists is meat. Start cooking one or two vegetarian meals every week and use veggies to bulk out meat stews, casseroles, stir fries and sauces – it's a healthier and cheaper way of eating.

How did it go?

Q I'm a single parent with one child living in a small flat – so it's difficult to take advantage of bargain bulk buys. We've got no where to store boxes of baked beans and jumbo packs of cereal, so how can we benefit?

A Why not try sharing a 'big' shop? Buy big and then split the food and the costs with friends or family. You could even take it in turns to do a run to the local cash and carry.

Q That's a good idea. Any other tips for smaller families?

A If you buy big packs of perishables like chicken breasts or minced meat, split them into smaller sized portions before you put them in the freezer. That way you can defrost as little or as much as you like at a time. It's always a good idea to freeze home-cooked dishes in individual or double portion sizes too, so you don't have to defrost a huge lasagne to feed two of you.

50
Perfect picnics

The secret of a stress-free, successful picnic is simplicity, plus careful planning and packing.

A picnic has to be the perfect family day out. Organise one to celebrate a sunny day, or as an excuse to catch up with old friends.

When it comes to picnic food, it doesn't pay to be too ambitious. Forget struggling with hot dishes, three courses, real plates and cutlery. Simple food that can be eaten with fingers works best.

Take advantage of the huge range of ready-made picnic products available and share the menu with other families.

KEEP IT COOL

- A large, insulated cool bag is absolutely essential for summer picnics. Many of the bigger supermarket branches give them away free with delicatessen purchases in the summer months – so look out for those.

Pack up individual bags of food for children and write their names on them – they'll love delving in to see what's inside. You could even include a cheap gift in each – a styrofoam glider or bottle of bubbles perhaps. Just make sure they're all the same to avoid squabbles.

- Reusable ice bricks are handy to keep food cool. Place them in the upper layers of your picnic box packing, rather than in the bottom, as cool air sinks. Even better than ice bricks, however, is to chill absolutely everything overnight, from sandwiches to drinks and fruit so they're nice and cold when you pack them.
- Airtight boxes are also a picnic must-have. Choose square or oblong boxes over round – they'll make it easier to stack more goodies in your cool bag.

WHAT TO EAT

Sandwiches

The picnic staple. Aim for two or three different fillings. Something simple and universally popular for the children (Marmite, ham, tuna, cheese and turkey are favourites) and a couple of more sophisticated fillings for adults. Choose thin- or medium-cut bread so they're not too bulky for little mouths.

- Always use butter or spread on bread, and take it right to the edges of the bread. That way there'll be a waterproof seal to stop the filling making the sandwiches soggy.
- Pack any salad garnishes such as tomato and cucumber slices or lettuce separately – to be added at the picnic itself. Salad tends to go flabby and make the sandwiches soggy very quickly. Personally I only ever make 'one filling' sandwiches and take a selection of veggies that can be eaten on the side with fingers instead – such as carrot, baby sweetcorn, cucumber and celery batons, cherry tomatoes etc.

- Ring the changes with tortilla wraps, pitta bread, bagels, foccacia and rolls.
- Sandwiches should be carefully wrapped in greaseproof paper or foil so they keep their shape, then packed snugly in an airtight box so they don't get squashed in transit.

Birthday party picnic? Read IDEA 46, *Party on*, for additional tips.

Try another idea…

Extra savouries

Small savoury items like cocktail sausages, small cubes of tortilla, mini Scotch eggs, sticks of cheese and small sausage rolls are all traditional children's picnic favourites. Choose one or two of these, then perhaps something bigger and more impressive for older children and adults – a quiche, perhaps, or a large pork pie, salmon *en croute* or tomato and goat's cheese tart. Don't forget to take a plate or board for it to stand on – and pre-slice or take a knife.

Crisps etc.

If these are to be shared by adults and children, avoid exotic crisps with obscure flavours and go instead for plain potato rings, cheesy puffs, bread sticks and cheese straws.

Fruit

A bit of preparation here means you won't be left with piles of skins, stones and cores that will attract wasps. Think de-stalked grapes (always slice them if smaller children are going

'We hope that, when the insects take over the world, they will remember with gratitude how we took them along on all our picnics.'
BILL VAUGHAN (1915–1977),
American journalist and author

Defining idea…

219

to eat them), trimmed and halved strawberries, peeled and segmented clementines, sliced peaches and nectarine or pineapple chunks.

The sweet stuff

Anything with chocolate is best avoided on hot days as it will melt almost as soon as it's out of the cool bag. Again opt for finger foods so there's no need for extra plates – or if you do take something that needs slicing, use napkins to serve it on. Good traditional choices are fairy cakes, fruit tarts, Battenburg, Victoria sponge. Gingerbread men and other children's biscuits go down well too – and are handy for going-home snacks when the children suddenly realise they've been too excited to eat much.

And finally, don't forget …

- Something to sit on.
- Something that will give shade if you have a baby with you.
- Black bin bags to take your rubbish away.
- Wipes for sticky fingers and muddy knees.
- Paper cups or reusable plastic glasses for drinks.
- Paper or reusable plastic plates for food.
- A ball (take an inflatable one to save space) or similar toy, to play with.
- A bottle opener – or choose screw cap bottles.
- A knife.
- A small first aid kit containing antiseptic wipes, plasters and sting-ease spray.
- Suncream, hats and long sleeves.
- A camera.

Q   Any ideas for picnic drinks?

How did it go?

A   *If the adults are having wine or Pimms, treat the children to their own picnic 'cocktails'. Add sliced fruit to pink lemonade or mix equal quantities of pure fruit smoothie with soda water. Make sure you take plenty of thirst-quenching plain water for the rest of the day too.*

Q   We always end up with lots of leftover picnic food. Is it OK to bring it all home again?

A   *You must throw perishables like deli items and sandwiches away I'm afraid. The longest time that vulnerable food can survive unrefrigerated is two hours – though really warm weather will reduce this limit to one hour. Dry goods like crisps, biscuits and cake (as long as it's not filled with cream) can come home with you – just make sure there's something clean and resealable to pack them in.*

51

The big freeze

Making friends with your freezer can help you produce a delicious home-cooked meal anytime.

If your freezer contains nothing more than a packet of fish fingers and a bag of frozen peas, then a little foresight can save you time and money in the long run.

Whether you're weaning your baby, have a fussy toddler with a variable appetite or need to feed school-age kids *now* – cooking in larger quantities and storing meals in the freezer can save a huge amount of time, money and stress.

WEANING FOODS

Babies eat such tiny quantities of food at first – it's well worth cooking up a couple of batches of fruit or vegetable purée and freezing them in ice-cube trays to defrost whenever you need them.

To make a purée: peel, core and chop your chosen fruit or veg then steam or boil in a little unsalted water until soft (do not add sugar to fruit). Drain, then purée in a blender – adding a little of the cooking water to get the right texture. Allow to

Here's an idea for you... **Where possible, use square and rectangular containers to store food in the freezer – they stack better and waste less space. Alternatively, pre-form liquids (or solids with liquids, such as stews) into square blocks. Pour the liquid into a polythene bag that is sitting inside a square-sided container. Freeze it like this, then remove the solid block from the container and seal the bag.**

cool, then pour into a sterilised ice cube tray and freeze. Once the purée is frozen, tip the individual cubes into a freezer bag, remove as much air as possible then seal. Be sure to write what's in the bag and date it. Fruit and vegetable purées will last for 6 months in a four star freezer.

MAIN MEALS

If you're making bolognese sauce, a stew, or even home-made chicken nuggets and burgers for supper – double the quantity and save some in the freezer. Here are the rules:

- Only freeze food that it is really fresh and in good condition. Handle it as little as possible before you freeze it.
- Never put foods that are still slightly warm into the freezer – it can cause the temperature to rise which may affect the other, already frozen foods you have stored in there. Ideally chill home-made food in the fridge before freezing.
- Pack and seal food with care. If food is exposed to moisture or cold air it can begin to deteriorate. Use special freezer bags available from supermarkets, freezer film, polythene bags, plastic containers, aluminium foil (heavy grade only and, if in doubt, double wrap). Don't use aluminium foil for acidic foods such as citrus fruits. Don't use thin cling film or glass. Exclude as much air from the container as possible before you put it in the freezer and label and date everything clearly.
- Freeze food in single or double portions. It freezes faster, takes less time to thaw and allows you to defrost the exact quantities you need.

- Leave a small amount of 'air space' in containers when freezing liquids like soups and stews, to allow for expansion.
- Interleave any foods like burgers and fishcakes that might otherwise stick together with pieces of greaseproof paper or freezer film.
- Consider how you want to cook the food before freezing it – don't freeze food in metal containers if you want to microwave it straight from the freezer.
- Never re-freeze food once it has thawed.
- Keep your freezer as full as possible (with a little space between items to allow cold air to circulate). Empty spaces need more energy to keep cool – if necessary add loaves of bread to fill up the yawning gaps.

If you're baking, make double quantities of cakes and biscuits and freeze for the next birthday party (cakes will keep for about 4 months in the freezer). See IDEA 46, *Party on*, for recipes.

Try another idea…

THAWING FOOD

Thawing frozen food must be done thoroughly and efficiently to ensure it's safe to eat.

- Never let food thaw in a warm environment – instead let it thaw out slowly in the fridge or thaw it in the microwave.
- Make absolutely sure large quantities of items are thoroughly thawed through before cooking.
- Cook food as soon as possible after it has thawed.
- Always cook thawed meals until they're piping hot all the way through.

'One morning, as I went to the freezer door, I asked my wife, "What should I take out for dinner?" Without a moment's hesitation, she replied, 'Me.''
ANONYMOUS

Defining idea…

225

How did it go?

Q   Our next-door neighbour has just given us loads of vegetables from his allotment. Any tips?

A   *Always freeze veggies as soon as possible after picking. Unless you're going to eat them within a few weeks, most vegetables keep better if they are blanched first.*

   Trim, shell, top and tail or slice veggies as you would normally, then freeze immediately or blanch by plunging into boiling water for one minute or 2–3 minutes for harder vegetables such as carrot and corn on the cob. Soft vegetables like courgettes and mange tout need just 10 seconds or so. Remove and plunge into iced water. Drain thoroughly and then pack your veg in 450g/1lb bags or boxes and freeze.

Q   I've a feeling we might get some fruit this year too ... what shall we do?

A   *Fruit that is suitable for freezing has to be ripe and in good condition. Small berries like raspberries and blueberries should be frozen individually. Spread the fruit out on a baking tray covered in greaseproof paper – freeze until solid, and then pack the fruit in freezer bags or cartons. Other fruit, such as apples, rhubarb, gooseberries and strawberries, are best cooked, sweetened and then frozen as fillings for pies and puddings.*

52

Petits gourmets

Challenge your child's palate with some unusual foods and flavours.

Whilst kids can be fussy eaters — they can also have some surprisingly grown-up tastes.

According to a recent British survey of 1,500 children aged 3–5, their favourite food is not, as you might suspect, chips or baked beans – but curry, closely followed by sweet and sour chicken. Yes, it appears even very young children have a taste for strongly flavoured food these days.

One theory, backed up by many baby experts, is that children pick up their tastes for various foods in their mother's womb and through the different flavours that permeate into breast milk. Perhaps it's no coincidence to discover, then, that the UK's favourite dish of all is chicken tikka masala.

I have a friend who adores garlic with everything. Possibly as a result of that, her son was popping whole pickled garlic cloves in his mouth like they were sweets at the age of 18 months. Another friend that craved olives during her pregnancy now has a

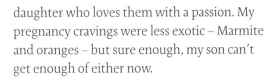

Here's an idea for you...
Take advantage of the recipe cards you can get in larger supermarkets. Let older children choose from a handful of unfamiliar recipe options that include some of their favourite foods. Buy the ingredients to create the dish and let them help you make it.

daughter who loves them with a passion. My pregnancy cravings were less exotic – Marmite and oranges – but sure enough, my son can't get enough of either now.

So perhaps one of the keys to raising an unfussy eater is to eat a varied diet – including plenty of the foods you want her to eat once she's older – particularly whilst you're pregnant and breast feeding.

Once a child is 12 months old and can eat more widely, don't be afraid to offer her new tastes. Many of us are guilty of serving nothing but 'safe', bland meals, because we're afraid anything too unusual may simply be rejected.

Remember, the broader her diet, the more likely she is to be getting all the nutrients she needs. Most children are naturally cautious about foods, so always offer one new food at a time and in small quantities.

And make it fun. Approach anything new with the attitude that you're giving her something delicious to try rather than timidly handing it over and waiting for her to turn up her nose. You may well be surprised by what she will accept and enjoy.

FOODS FOR THOUGHT

Everything starts with the shopping trip. To challenge your child's tastebuds, take her shopping with you. Encourage her to choose one 'new' food item that's not on the regular list to take home and try every week. For example:

If she's a timid eater, start off with something really simple – like letting her choose a new pasta shape, breakfast cereal or dessert. The stipulation is, it has to be a variety she hasn't tried before.

If she's a little braver, fruit doesn't have to mean bananas and grapes. Lychees, kumquats, star fruit, cape gooseberries, pomegranates, guava, custard apple, passion fruit and papaya can all be found in large supermarkets at different times of the year. Let your child choose an unusual fruit to be shared by the family for dessert.

If your child only associates cheese with the words 'triangle' or 'string', it's time to give something more challenging a go. Most supermarket deli counters will let you sample several cheeses at quieter times of the day. Have a taste session and let your child choose which cheese you'll all be eating that week.

All kids love sausages, so try swapping your regular chipolatas for one of the more interesting varieties flavoured with sundried tomatoes, garlic or cranberry. Again, allow her to decide which it's to be.

Try another idea…

To find out how to cook and serve another fun dish – 'salmon in a bag' – turn to IDEA 34, *Fishing for compliments*.

Defining idea…

'**Exciting food should exercise the senses and stretch the palate.**'
ALAN WONG, restaurateur and cookery writer

229

Take a look at the herbs and spices. Let your child pick the most interesting one she can find and then work a recipe around it later in the week.

Visit the fish counter or meat section and pick a new type of fish, seafood or meat to try. Many young children seem to love smoked salmon, prawns and liver.

TABLE TALK

How you serve food is important too. If meals in your house tend to be meat or fish and two veg, or a simple bowl of pasta – start thinking about making things a little more exciting and challenging occasionally.

Fondues are great fun for older children. Cook meat in hot oil or dip bread in cheese sauce. Cut up some exotic fruit and make a chocolate dip for a special occasion.

Kebab skewers are fun way to present food too. Thread them with barbecue ingredients such as chicken and peppers or cold salad items such as mozzarella balls and cherry tomatoes or fruit and marshmallows.

Make a stir fry and eat it from bowls with chopsticks.

Q   **We're not big curry eaters in our household – but would like to try a family takeaway. Which curries are suitable for children?**

How did it go?

A   *If your child is over 12 months, I would choose a chicken curry to start off with – perhaps a korma, which usually contains ground almonds, coconut and cream. Pasanda, which also often contains almonds, along with puréed tomatoes and cream is another pretty good choice as is tikka masala – which is usually spicy but not hot.*

Q   **What else should I order?**

A   *Plain boiled rice, plain naan and some veggie side dishes such as onion bhajis and raitha, a cooling yogurt dip. The spiciness of foods from different restaurants can vary widely, however – so it's probably a good idea to ask them to make some recommendations or keep the dishes mild for you when you order.*

The end...

Or is it a new beginning?

We hope that the ideas in this book will have inspired you to try some new ways to get your children to eat good food. We hope you've found some great health tips and sneaky short cuts and that you're already expanding your repertoire, getting organised and being more aware of what your children are eating. You should be well on your way to having healthier, more satisfied and happier kids.

So why not let us know all about it? Tell us how you got on. What did it for you – what had them coming back for seconds, every meal? Maybe you've got some tips of your own you want to share (see next page if so). And if you liked this book you may find we have even more brilliant ideas that could change other areas of your life for the better.

You'll find the Infinite Ideas crew waiting for you online at www.infideas.com.

Or if you prefer to write, then send your letters to:
Healthy cooking for children
The Infinite Ideas Company Ltd
36 St Giles, Oxford, OX1 3LD, United Kingdom

We want to know what you think, because we're all working on making our lives better too. Give us your feedback and you could win a copy of another *52 Brilliant Ideas* book of your choice. Or maybe get a crack at writing your own.

Good luck. Be brilliant.

Offer one

CASH IN YOUR IDEAS

We hope you enjoy this book. We hope it inspires, amuses, educates and entertains you. But we don't assume that you're a novice, or that this is the first book that you've bought on the subject. You've got ideas of your own. Maybe our author has missed an idea that you use successfully. If so, why not put it in an email and send it to: yourauthormissedatrick@infideas.com, and if we like it we'll post it on our bulletin board. Better still, if your idea makes it into print we'll send you four books of your choice. or the cash equivalent. You'll be fully credited so that everyone knows you've had another Brilliant Idea.

Offer two

HOW COULD YOU REFUSE?

Amazing discounts on bulk quantities of Infinite Ideas books are available to corporations, professional associations and other organisations.

For details call us on:
+44 (0)1865 514888
fax: +44 (0)1865 514777
or e-mail: info@infideas.com

Where it's at ...

FREE book offer

Thank you for buying this book. We hope you enjoyed it and found lots of useful tips and have already been able to put them into practice. You can now improve another area of your life by taking advantage of our fabulous FREE book offer.* Does your relationship need some work or could you do with untangling that jungle you call your garden but aren't sure where to start? Perhaps you just want some tips on living a happier, healthier life. Once you've decided what you'd like to try, getting hold of your free book is simple. Look down the list below and decide which title you'd like to receive FREE of charge. Then either fill in the coupon and send it to the address below or call up and quote your unique offer code, giving the title of the book you would like to receive. Choose from the titles below:

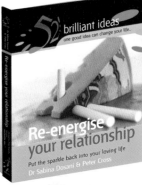

- [ ] *Blooming pregnancy*
- [ ] *Create your dream garden*
- [ ] *Live longer*
- [ ] *Perfect parties*
- [ ] *Perfect weddings*
- [ ] *Re-energise your relationship*
- [ ] *Survive divorce*
- [ ] *Unleash your creativity*
- [ ] *Web sites that work*
- [ ] *Whole health*

How to place your order

Name: ....

Delivery address: ....

....

E-mail: ....

Telephone: ....

We never give details to third parties nor will we bombard you with lots of junk mail!

By post: Fill in all the relevant details, cut this page out (or photocopy it) and send it to: Infinite Ideas, 36 St Giles, Oxford OX1 3LD

Over the telephone: Call +44 (0) 1865 514 888.
Please quote your unique offer code.

Any questions please call +44 (0) 1865 514 888 or e-mail info@infideas.com.

infinite ideas
www.52brilliantideas.com

238

For full details of these books and others in the **52 Brilliant Ideas** series please visit **www.52brilliantideas.com.**

*This offer is available to UK residents only wh stocks last.